GRAB
MORE
MARKET
SHARE

GRAB
MORE
MARKET
SHARE

HOW TO **WRANGLE BUSINESS**
AWAY FROM
LAZY COMPETITORS

ROSS SHAFER

WILEY

John Wiley & Sons, Inc.

For general information on our other products and services or for technical support, please contact our Customer Care Department within the United States at (800) 762-2974, outside the United States at (317) 572-3993 or fax (317) 572-4002.

Wiley also publishes its books in a variety of electronic formats. Some content that appears in print may not be available in electronic books. For more information about Wiley products, visit our web site at www.wiley.com.

ISBN 978-1-118-13004-9 (cloth); ISBN 978-1-118-14544-9 (ebk); ISBN 978-1-118-14545-6 (ebk); ISBN 978-1-118-14546-3 (ebk)

Printed in the United States of America

10 9 8 7 6 5 4 3 2 1

This book is dedicated to my father, Chuck Shafer (1927–2001). My father was more than a survivor; he welcomed change and was an early adopter in every sense of the word. He was fascinated with new cars, new cities and towns, new technology, and friends who could teach him new ideas. And he did it all without any hidden agenda.

My dad was a man of the highest integrity, manners, and sense of adventure. He held a multitude of positions and titles throughout his life: crop dusting pilot, car salesman, man who built his own aerobatic airplane, thirty-second-degree Mason, and beloved executive with ARCO. Yet he took the most pride in being as much fun as any neighbor could be.

When he passed away in 2001, my mother gave me a large box containing about a hundred handwritten cards and letters from his "fans." A lot of people (most of whom we didn't even know) detailed his kind acts and warm remembrances. Seriously, complete strangers recounted good deeds that my mother and I never knew about. For 71 years, my dad had been sneaking around behind our backs...being a nice guy.

Though I hadn't predicted it—or intended for it to happen—many of my dad's life lessons kept surfacing as I was studying dozens of organizations for fresh growth practices in a tough economy. The survivor who was my father still resonates in other people's actions and success.

I wish I could thank you in person, Pop!

Contents

Acknowledgments

I have read about writers who sit alone (usually in a wooded cabin) and without outside influence, are able to drain their brains of every last drop of imagination, experience, and inspiration. Six months later they emerge with a masterpiece. I'm not that guy. I need to soak up the world . . . to see what the current culture is up to. I read books, blogs, and I am a self-confessed news junkie. But my primary source of inspiration comes from the people I meet on my speaking engagements. I learn something inspirational from every job. That's why networking is so important at a corporate meeting: because somebody somewhere has invented or adopted a fresh practice that has kept their business vital . . . and scared the devil out of their competitors. I revel in the simple innovations created not by brain trusts or think tanks but rather by the seemingly ordinary people who are trying to meet payrolls during challenging economic times. So to the many men and women I've met on the road who found a way to dominate their industries against staggering odds, I thank you for allowing me to eavesdrop on your ideas and letting me share them with the readers of this book.

Since I don't have a writer's cabin—and because I don't want to end up like James Caan in the film *Misery*—I write from my home office. So I especially need to thank my loving wife, Leah, for allowing me to stay holed up in there while I sift and sort this stuff out. It's hard for Leah because she is quite busy herself—yet does her best to keep our active five-year old daughter, Lauren

(Lolo), at bay while I'm mulling. Often, just when I've finally crystallized a thought and am anxious to get it down on paper, Lolo will get on the house intercom (which blares in my office) to ask if I can meet her in her room to hear a new song or play pet shop. I usually accommodate her; which is why *my* books take longer to write than, say, Tolstoy's.

I also want to thank my business partners, Cam Marston and Helen Broder. You two are my sounding boards and vent pipes. Your judgment is always more sound and less emotional than my own so I am grateful to have you in my life. Special thanks go to my other partner, Keith Harrell. Keith was my brother in this business and a daily source of inspiration. After you saw Keith—or talked to him on the phone—he always made you feel better about yourself. Keith and I are both from Seattle. We were both college athletes. And, we both gravitated toward speaking and writing as adults. God took Keith home last year, and still I think about him—and use his advice—every day.

Speaking of partners, I must thank the folks at John Wiley & Sons. Kudos go to Lauren Murphy, who has shepherded this project. And many thanks go to the editing team of Christine Moore, Deborah Schindlar, and Chris Furry. It takes a lot of people to decipher what I write.

Finally, I have to acknowledge my two fine sons, Adam and Ryan Shafer. They did not directly contribute to this book but they gave me less worry when they both married wonderful women, Holli and Anh, respectively. As the flower girl in their weddings, Little Lolo loves to brag about her two new sisters.

Leaders, Read This First

You are a leader charged with directing your company (or division) back to prosperity following what many have called a debilitating recession.

How will you inspire your people?

When will you start spending or investing capital again? Where will you spend that money?

What new tools and metrics do you need to be competitive—not only in your market—but in retaining and managing talent?

Is it true what you keep hearing, "This is the new normal"?

Who can you turn to for advice?

Humility aside, I'm one of the guys you should call. Throughout the recession—and now well into the recovery—I've spoken at more than 200 national and international business conferences. I've covered banking, manufacturing, insurance, high-tech, diverse services, pharmaceutical, retail, transportation, and government.

I was hired to reveal the research and cross-pollinated fresh practices I've unveiled at competing organizations. The results cast a spotlight on the innovative market share winners . . . as well as the lazy and unchanging has-beens.

Now that the new economy's flatline is starting to show encouraging blips of a strengthening pulse, skepticism and optimism are trying to establish wedded bliss by maintaining a compatible balance. Your stakeholders are in love with your drive and enthusiasm—but they want deliverables from you. Right here. Right now. If you get this right, the rewards will astound your spouse and your parents.

What you will read in this book is my hit list of those fresh practices that caused nimble organizations to wrangle market share away from their lazy competitors.

Unabashedly, those innovative and nimble organizations are positioning themselves to dominate their markets *after* the recovery.

As you go through these examples and case studies, remember that even though the global recession temporarily paralyzed growth, along with creating double-digit unemployment, the world did not shut down. Agile, culture-aware organizations continued to seduce market share away from their frightened, ill-equipped, and often sleepy competitors.

—Ross Shafer

GRAB
MORE
MARKET
SHARE

Chapter 1

First, You Must Attack Market Share

Are You Merely Striving for Average?

D o you want to settle for 1 to 2 percent growth in the recovery?

Even the best-informed economists believe the current market may grow at a rate of between 1 and 2 percent. That's hardly a snapback recovery, is it? But will your stakeholders and board members settle for 1 percent? Of course they won't.

What if your particular segment happens to be in a declining market? That is to say, demand for what you sell is declining. Should you give up; simply roll over and blame the economy or the competition? No, you shouldn't; that would be ridiculous. If you want to grow in a slowly recovering economy, a stagnant economy, or even a declining market, your best—and truly, *only*—plan is to "steal" market share from your competitors.

Maybe you don't like the word *steal* and prefer to use *win*. Whatever term you use, know that your survival depends on wrestling business away from other companies that do what you do and provide what you provide.

This is a lesson we learned from none other than fast-food linchpin McDonald's. The company noticed there was probably a wild growth opportunity in the specialty coffee and smoothie business and that people were increasingly enamored of places like Starbucks and Juice It Up, which were growing at impressive rates. Though McDonald's had actually tested its McCafé concept many years earlier, the company didn't officially launch the initiative until early 2009. By doing so, it charged Starbucks full bore, and Starbucks had already begun to cut prices in some markets due to the economy. McDonald's, which saw and took advantage of the vulnerability in Starbucks' market share, acted on a fundamental truth: Capitalizing on a competitor's weakness is always a solid recovery strategy. McDonald's plan was to roll out the McCafé concept to 11,000 of the company's 14,000 locations, with a goal of pulling in a projected $1 billion in revenue. It worked. In the second quarter of 2010, McDonald's raked in $420 million, thereby making its billion-dollar target a reality.

It's important for you to absorb the fact that McDonald's did not *create* a fresh billion dollars in coffee consumption. Rather, it *stole* a staggering amount of business from Starbucks and other coffee specialty stores. Starbucks felt the pressure and, in 2009, closed more than 270 locations.

Subway, with its 34,000 sandwich locations, was also paying attention to these latest developments and decided accordingly to venture into the breakfast business. Since Subway already had most of the necessary ingredients to make sandwiches, it just added English muffins and eggs. Subway, too, was hoping to grab an additional revenue stream of $1 billion. I was at a launch meeting for this concept, and the hushed murmur making its way through the managerial crowd was, "If we start selling breakfast sandwiches, does that mean we have to get to the store an hour earlier?" I said to myself, "Yeah—but isn't an hour earlier worth an extra billion dollars!?"

A regional director of that chain told me during a recent phone call, "Revenue hasn't [climbed] quite as high as we'd hoped, but [this move] proved we could be nimble and react to our market's needs. Adding breakfast was a very smart move for us . . . although I do have to go to bed a little earlier these days."

Moving from the food service industry to online retail, we have to admire Zappos.com as a pure model of a company that came to the industry late, yet ramped up its quest to gobble market share. You are probably aware of the Zappos story by now; if you're not, it's fair to say that Zappos.com is the Amazon.com of the retail shoe business. The company started in 1999 with a fairly simply business model: to sell shoes over the Internet. Given that most people (at that time) liked to try on a lot of different shoes in the relative safety of a retail store ("I don't want these . . . but *these*"), ordering shoes over the web— sight unseen and foot unfelt—wasn't an easy behavior to change. Nonetheless, by being overly customer focused, Zappos.com grew from zero to a billion-dollar-plus shoe company in just 10 years.

Again, Zappos.com didn't convince consumers to buy an *additional* billion dollars' worth of shoes. The company recognized that some of its largest competitors assumed that *they* had the discount shoe market cornered. Hubris always makes a competitor vulnerable. Zappos.com identified its softest targets and stole the business from formerly worthy competitors. To wit, Payless ShoeSource had closed 218 stores by 2009.

Guess what else happened? Zappos.com was purchased by the company that inspired its business model. In July 2009, Amazon.com bought Zappos for $928 million.

The same take-it-from-your-competition strategy was used by home electronics industry behemoth Best Buy. Recognizing that its largest competitor, Circuit City, had a customer service Achilles' heel, Best Buy painted its target and devised a strategy. Through a studied regimen of offering extreme customer service—and by installing a new employee work model (called ROWE, which we'll discuss in detail later in this book)—Best Buy applied so much market pressure that Circuit City was forced to shut down 567 stores. Others fell as well: Sam Goody buttoned

up 340 locations, and Good Guys lost 71. Even Crazy
Eddie succumbed, with more than 40 closures. Best Buy
performed a serious, tactical theft of market share that
resulted in significant and lasting company growth.

Who Says Geeks are Meek?

The companies who specialize in computer data storage,
storage clouds, visualization, and so on, work in what
some call a brutally competitive, one trillion dollar market.
Leaders in this industry include EMC, IBM, Hitachi Data
Systems, 3PAR, NetApp, Brocade, and at least a dozen
others. But don't kid yourself. These companies are on
fire; some growing from 20 to 50 percent in 2010. With that
much money at stake, these storage sharks can smell blood
several continents away.

I attended a meeting where Data Storage Company "A"
announced, without apology, that they were targeting the
biggest money customers in the world—and laying out the
tactics necessary to win market share from giant Data
Storage Companies A, B, C, D, and E. They had grown
nearly 30 percent during the recession and were intent
upon world domination. They also wanted to emphasize
extreme customer attention matters . . . in that their current
clients were equally vulnerable to a takeover.

As an example, a senior executive told the crowd of
2,000 salespeople that Data Storage Company "B" had
been taking "secret" meetings with one of Storage Company "A's" biggest customers. When Storage Company
"A" found out, they went to Defcon 1 (in military terms,
Defcon 1 is the highest level of defense: it literally means
"pistol cocked—war is imminent"). Company "A" took
this threat seriously and were not about to lose this major
customer without a fight.

Company "A" calmly got their client to give them a grace period to defend their work. During this time-out, Company "A" put 20 of their smartest people in a room to hammer out what it would take to retain the business. No ethics were breached. Just plain old-fashioned shoulder-to-shoulder creativity and high-level honing of their value proposition. After all, this was war.

In the end, Storage Company "A" was able to keep the client. But it was a blaring $100 million dollar wake up call for them to remain ever vigilant and informed about their clients' needs. (And, when possible, be more anticipatory.)

For you, this is an object lesson in exactly how fragile your market can be. There are no guarantees your best customer and clients will stay with you forever. Their needs change. Sometimes overnight. Their management team may change and old friends like working with old friends. If your clients detect even a tinge of feelings taken for granted (or unloved by you) they *will* listen to your competitor's offer.

Please insist that your sales team read this story. The longevity of your company and their individual pay-checks depend upon retaining hard won customers. We can never be complacent with people who pay us money because in order to score more market share it's not enough to take business away from a competitor. You must be ready to competitively defend your reason for living—so you don't grow lazy enough to lose your invaluable current clients.

Grabbing Share Is *Not* a Cakewalk

In all of the preceding cases, the organizations that ac-quired more market share took the process very seriously and approached it very deliberately. Each one started with a financial target and identified specific competitors. They knew the realistic size of the opportunity. They designed a timeline, a strategy, and a set of variable tactics to take some of that business away from their competitors.

However, it's equally critical to understand that even the best-executed plans don't *automatically* win market share. No matter what the strategy, they have to *earn* the business. In order to do so, the winners had to do a better job than their competitors with regard to customers, team members, products, services, marketing—and keep themselves open to course corrections when new information became available.

Chapter 2 offers a more surgical approach. You'll learn exactly who and what you need to study in order to get more market share. But for now, let's build a foundation.

Homework

- Which of your competitors have a vulnerable market share?
- What is a realistic percentage increase you could expect?
- What would be the projected timeline to accomplish such a "heist"?
- How much overall revenue would that percentage of market share represent?
- How much will it cost you in cash, workers, and other resources to achieve that percentage?
- Can you get the rest of your team on board? If not, what can you do to convince them? (Here's an idea: Send them this book!)

Chapter 2

Don't Let the Culture Embarrass You

Power to the People

The collective public consciousness (aka, the *culture*) is the entity that ultimately decides whether a given venture will succeed or fail. As a group, *these people* determine whether a music CD is a hit; *they* decide whether a book becomes a best seller; and *they* dictate which motion pictures become box office smash hits.

The public, the culture, the collective thinking of a lot of people also decide whether the goods and services you sell will become popular. If what you sell is popular, it is in demand. It becomes relevant and important to *them*. Your company will grow when *they* rush out and tell their friends.

Organizations that strive to remain relevant to their clients, suppliers, customers, and employees will always weather an economic crisis better than those that disregard the world around them. Being relevant means you *matter* to them. If you don't matter, you can go out of business and nobody will care—or possibly even notice.

I wrote a lot about this bullheaded phenomenon in my book *Are You Relevant?* It is incomprehensible to me that a number of once successful (and really smart) companies go profit-blind by refusing to change. *Profit-blindness* is a term I assign to an organization that has made a lot of money doing something one way (usually the original way) but that is so stupidly complacent in its success that it ignores the obvious culture changes that can put it out of business. Our culture is constantly rewriting the rules that determine how customers want to buy and how employees want to work. As much as I despise clichés, "You snooze, you lose" is a classic worth tattooing on your forehead. And, worse than *any* cliché, I hate hearing, "But that's the way we've always done things."

Trends Never Sneak Up On Anybody

I want to walk you through this, not to be condescending, but to make sure you know exactly what you're looking for. You have to stay relevant, to still *matter* to your customers and coworkers, or you run the risk of becoming extinct. At that point, nobody will care. Staying relevant only happens when you continue to innovate. The logic of staying relevant through innovation is so important I want to burn that credo into your working subconscious. Innovation is your baseline for grabbing market share away from your competition.

Q: *How* do I know what to innovate?
A: You pay attention to the culture.
Q: *What* do I innovate?
A: The culture will tell you. Actually, they will scream it at you.
Q: *When* do I pay attention to the culture?
A: Every day.
Q: *What* am I looking for?
A: Trends.
Q: *What* is a trend?
A: A *trend* is a new way of thinking that captures the public's consciousness.
Q: *What* is a definition of *public consciousness*?
A: It's when a lot of people start changing their habits all at once.
Q: *How* will we know when the public consciousness has caused a habit change?

A: You will see news stories on TV or the web. You'll hear your friends talk about it on Facebook. Your children will tell you. You'll read about it in your magazines. Celebrities will start talking about it.

Organizations love to overthink strategy and tactics; however, innovation does not require a complicated formula. At the core of your success, you must accept that if you ignore the public consciousness, *they* have the power and influence to ignore *you*—or worse, erase you from existence.

However, if you create a plan to leverage the public consciousness, *they* have the power to make you wealthy and famous.

The Video Store Lesson

We all believed that Blockbuster and Hollywood Video had vastly improved our lives during the 1990s—and we admired the phenomenal business models they used to do so. Watching movies at home gave birth to the home theater revolution that allowed us to rent the latest box office movies as VHS tapes without having to buy the $99 video. But then something interesting happened. The digitization of movies radically *decreased* the size of the movie box, making it possible for a new company (enter Netflix) to mail the DVDs directly to us. We watched the DVD and sent it back, postage paid. We didn't even have to leave our homes!

The next thing we knew, Hollywood Video filed for bankruptcy, and Blockbuster, with over a billion dollars in debt, followed suit soon after. Was Netflix so small it was able to fly under the radar—and sneak up on Blockbuster and Hollywood Video?

Nope.

Netflix started in 1999 because the founder was a guy like you and me who was tired of being charged late fees by video rental stores. He created a company that allowed us to stay in our jammies and order videos that came in the mail. Then in 2000, Netflix changed to a flat-fee subscription service that gave users the chance for unlimited rentals without due dates, late fees, shipping or handling fees, or per-title rental fees.

Today, Netflix offers DVDs both by snail mail and by streaming movies online to (are you ready?) more than *14 million subscribers!*

This trend didn't sneak up on anybody. The Netflix business model wasn't a secret. The collective public consciousness (i.e., *everyone*) was talking about it. By 2002, Netflix was mailing 190,000 discs a day and had almost 700,000 loyal subscribers. This trend was so blatantly obvious that apparently only the two giants in the industry where it was occurring chose to ignore it. Anyone who ever rented a movie saw the proverbial writing on the wall. The traditional video store was entering the Ice Age. Still, it took almost a decade to turn Blockbuster and Hollywood Video into dinosaurs. In October 2007, Hollywood Video's parent company (Movie Gallery, Inc.) filed for Chapter 11 bankruptcy. By September 2010, Blockbuster was bankrupt as well.

Netflix owes its success to a culture that was essentially begging for a change. Before Netflix, everyone complained about late fees; we just didn't know what to do about it. When a company that offered an alternative came along, we all jumped at the chance to use it.

Second, the public consciousness saw the improved picture quality of the DVD and began buying the machines by the millions. The smaller size of a DVD allowed for easy mailing. Next, the digital format (instead of VHS tapes) made it possible to convert movies to binary code, making it possible to deliver movies via online streaming. This process eliminated postage, handling, and the potential for physical theft for both the consumer and Netflix. It's critical to note that, in the end, consumers voted Netflix into office with their wallets.

Your organization can learn this from the Netflix example: It doesn't matter how big, experienced, and successful your company is. If the public thinks your competitor's offering is better than yours, the public—and therefore, your competitor—will win.

The Music Industry Ignored an Obvious Trend. Apple Didn't

A similar misstep was made by formerly dominant music companies like Sony, Universal, Columbia, DreamWorks, A&M records, and others. The big dogs of music were partying like it was 1999—especially *in* 1999. Traditional CD producers and manufacturers owned the best artists, the most comprehensive distribution channels, and the best promotional vehicles. Artists like Mariah Carey, Robbie Robertson, and Whitney Houston were signing record deals worth $80 million to $125 million dollars.

In June of that same year, 20-year-olds Shawn Fanning and Sean Parker were developing a file sharing software program that would allow college students to freely trade MP3 music files. They called it Napster. Fanning and Parker knew all too well that there is nothing more appealing than free music to a college student (unless it's free beer coupled with free music).

Napster, of course, went viral. At its peak, the tool had 25 million users sharing 80,000 million songs. Of course, the artists who wrote the music considered this so-called sharing to be *stealing*. Lawsuits were numerous and usually successful, since copyright violations *had* taken place. Despite appeals, the Ninth Circuit court shut Napster down in July 2001.

While Napster had lost the fight, it had unequivocally derailed—and therefore transformed—the music industry. Listening to music via an MP3 sounded just as good as the CD. Even better, it meant that listeners could arrange their music in the order *they* preferred to hear it. Plus, they didn't have to buy an artist's entire album if what they really wanted was just one or two songs.

Today, the iPod is ubiquitous. You might even have three of four of them yourself. But the idea of a portable music player wasn't new. Remember the Walkman? Sony launched that portable tape player back in 1979. Given the obvious global success of the MP3 file, one would assume that Sony would be waiting in the wings with its superior version of an MP3 player once the Napster dust cleared.

But it wasn't. Seduced by the investment in its aging paradigm, Sony waited too long to change gears.

On the other hand, Apple was in the computer business, and while it didn't know anything about how the music business worked, it did know that the culture—our collective consciousness—had spoken. The direction in which we wanted to head was clear. Apple just had to create a device and way for artists to be paid.

While the record companies were fumbling about, trying to figure out how to save their CD businesses, Apple was experimenting with a new kind of MP3 player. Apple knew there had to be a store (virtual or otherwise) that would eventually pay an appropriate amount of money to the recording artist. The company also knew that consumers wanted to listen to music in a user-determined fashion.

The first iPod debuted in October 2001. It held 1,000 songs and had a scroll wheel so users could find and play the exact song they wanted. The price tag was an outrageous $400. Yet an eager public stood in long lines to purchase one.

Apple had revolutionized the music industry forever, leaving the traditional music companies glassy-eyed, overstaffed, and lost.

Was this a head-snapping trend that took the music industry completely by surprise? How *could* it? Isn't Sony one of the world's technology leaders? Napster shared millions of MP3s beginning in 1999, and the first iPod wasn't introduced until October 2001. Seriously, the iPod didn't arrive until two years *after* the shared MP3 file had already announced itself as the future.

C'mon. *Two years?*

The music industry should have been nimble enough to recognize that the tide was turning. It should have noticed a sea change like this. I mean, *you* would have noticed something like that in *your* industry, right? (Nod your head up and down.)

Kodak Should Have Kept the Shutter Open

I was attending a Kodak sales meeting circa 1999 when I heard a seasoned Kodak executive addressing a group of shaken salespeople. They were feeling shaken because they were getting a lot of heat from their customers about "digital photography." Kodak's customers were scared that the future of photo labs might be in jeopardy. I nearly popped a contact lens when I heard an executive blurt, "I know a lot of you are [becoming] concerned about digital photography—but don't be. It's just a fad that will interest early adopters."

How Could They Just Stand By and Watch?

What makes this entire scenario particularly startling is the fact that Kodak actually had a prototype for the world's first digital camera in 1975. However, the company waited until 1998 to reluctantly enter the consumer market. This debacle wasn't simply a matter of Kodak ignoring a new trend; indeed, the company was ignoring a revolutionary trend that *it* had invented!

Meanwhile, comparatively small calculator and wrist-watch company Casio took a chance on changing the collective consciousness by launching the first consumer-friendly digital camera in 1995. In May 1996, Canon paid attention and raised the bar with the PowerShot 600. By September of that year, Olympus jumped in with its D-300L (which had a mere 0.08 megapixel).

By 1998, the field was on fire. Digital cameras from Canon, Agfa, Hewlett-Packard, Leica, Olympus, Minolta, Sony Cyber-shot, Fujifilm, Casio, Epson, Ricoh, Toshiba, and Nikon flooded the market; even Kodak introduced a couple of models. However, the Kodak models didn't seem to get the same press interest as the other manufacturers—largely because (in my opinion, at least) Kodak's heart wasn't in it. Maybe Kodak still wasn't convinced that consumer digital photography was anything more than a fad. After all, the bulk of its massive profits still came from selling film.

You probably know the rest of the story. Digital photography changed the world. Instant images can be viewed, manipulated, e-mailed, faxed, PDF'd, converted to video, and uploaded as YouTube-ready movies via millions of cell phones. What is even more incredible is that an inexpensive 2011 cell phone has better megapixel quality than a high-end portrait studio camera from 1999.

Finally, abandoning denial in January 2004, Kodak announced it would no longer sell 35mm reloadable film in the United States, Canada, and Western Europe, but would still sell film in what it considered to be emerging markets—China, India, Eastern Europe, and Latin America. That decision indicated Kodak's market share was declining.

Although the company tried licensing Vivitar to manufacture cameras under the Kodak banner, by 2007, it was no longer licensing or manufacturing any film camera with the Kodak name. Kodak was essentially forced to focus on growth in the digital markets. Imagine that—one of the world leaders in film and film cameras since 1892 had to play catch-up in the industry it effectively invented.

How could this happen to such a great company? Didn't Kodak notice that the Fotomat booths that once peppered the American landscape with 4,000 kiosks in 1980 (all selling Kodak film) were quickly evaporating? Again, this trend was not a secret. The digital revolution was a movement hiding in plain sight.

Kodak's foot-dragging was a result of attempting to milk the blind profits generated by the celluloid film business. Apparently, the company wanted to run the demand well completely dry before venturing into "unknown" territory—the same territory it had introduced. Kodak ignored the golden rule of innovation: Innovate *before* you have to. Kodak had the technology, but it *didn't* innovate until it was too late.

To my mind, Kodak is a sad tale of American ingenuity crippled by self-imposed hibernation. At its peak in 1988, Kodak employed 143,000 people. Today, only about 20,000 full-timers collect a paycheck from Kodak. I have a friend who has worked at Kodak for 10 years. He has seen the workforce shrink from 78,000 in the year 2001 to the current level of 20,000 in 2011. I asked him if he still likes the company. He was gleeful, "Oh yeah, I love it! I know almost everybody." Good for the employees, perhaps, but not a great situation for a company once considered the leader in its field.

That Kindle Thing

By now, you all know about the Kindle e-reader. You may also know that it is estimated that nearly 1,000,000 books are available in an electronic format. Hey, right now you might be reading this book on your personal computer, your smart phone, a Kindle, an iPad, a Nook, an Intel Reader, an Aluratek e-reader, a Sony Daily Edition, or any number of hand-held devices. E-reading has caught on.

There is no question that reading books this way is a permanent shift in cultural behavior. I liken it to when people used to posit that rap music was a fad. Rap didn't go away and neither will the e-reader. What causes a fad to sustain is ongoing demand and rampant profitability. In fact, in July 2010, Amazon reported that for every 100 hardcover books sold, they were selling 180 Kindle editions of the same titles. In the paperback arena, Kindle editions sell 115 copies to every 100 copies of traditional paperback books. What is even more impressive about this shift is that Amazon was able to change the culture in less than four years from its launch of the first Kindle product in November 2007!

So does this mean that our beloved neighborhood bookstores will close down? Are the lazy days of strolling through a bookstore to manhandle a crisply minted new book over? For some, yes.

Borders filed for bankruptcy and is expected to close over 200 of its 674 stores. However, Barnes & Noble continue to survive; largely in part to the development of its own e-reader, the Nook. Hudson's 66 airport bookstore locations still make a strong showing throughout North America because weary travelers need something to do on layovers.

And, of course, many of us cherish the tactile qualities of a real book. We enjoy the heft and smell. We can flip to any page we like. And we can put it back on our (openly public) bookshelf to show our friends we have read it. Real books have yet another remarkable everlasting benefit. They never need recharging.

But rather than adopt the fear that e-reading will replace books, I prefer to think it has the potential to increase and restore an interest in reading. In many cases I own the same titles as both real books and e-books. I can see where the reduced cost of a Kindle edition would make books more accessible to students, the elderly, and even budget-minded vacationers. As you see with your work-related documents, we live in a world where both paper and digital can coexist peacefully. Stationery will never go away. People will still send greeting cards. The more I think about it, the more I doubt a doctor would ever frame a thumb drive containing his diploma.

There is a historical element surrounding electronic books that nobody talks about. The first e-reader was introduced by Sony in 1990. The Sony Data Discman—and the subsequent Sony Bookman—were CD-ROM driven devices that cost about $900. Astronomic price aside, the major detractors included the limited amount of content available back then, the short battery life, the screen resolution, and the weight (about two pounds). Still, there was demand! Sony could have been quick to address the size and battery issues (and determined how to capture a million book titles) and figured out how to sell them economically. Sony was a respected brand at the forefront of a reading revolution. Yet, they let the hungry amateurs in the market outperform them. Didn't they learn anything from the cultural beating they took from the Walkman's showdown with the iPod?

Homework

◆ What trend or trends are you ignoring? Are they trends that may be hiding in plain sight?

◆ What are your competitors offering today that they didn't offer two years ago? Is this any indication of what *you* should be offering? (Hint: The answer is probably yes.)

◆ Are you so profit-blinded by your old (successful) business model that you aren't paying attention to the next big thing?

◆ Are you willing to phase out your old business model?

◆ How quickly can you enter the trending market?

◆ Are you doing an exhaustive study on the trend instead of jumping into the game right away?

◆ What will a new business model cost in cash? Workers? Other resources?

◆ Do you need to sell an emerging trend up the line to management? If so, use the case studies in this book as a means of getting the C-suite managers on board.

Chapter 3

They Want Customer *Urgency . . . Not* Customer Service

Human Behavior Shifts Like Sand

P art of our personal company mission has been to track the evolution of the customers' needs and wants. And, brother, it's a moving target.

We have chronicled that human behavior shifts are influenced by two reliable factors: technology change and significant social events. Just as the 2011 earthquake in Japan literally reassigned the earth's axis, technology and social events can tweak the customer's behavioral axis.

Since 1994, we've been producing human resource training films, writing books, creating seminars and doing live breakout training. We work hard at this endeavor but freely admit that we are never finished learning. We use every session to advance the edict, "If you don't like change, you are really going to hate extinction."

While most organizations willingly accept this credo in regard to emerging technology, far too many forget to apply it to the art of customer care and feeding. Customer service needs change at the same pace as customers' attitudes and habits evolve.

Since the purpose of this little book is to increase the velocity of your ability to adapt to fresh practices, you must know that one size does *not* fit all. Customer service means different things to different people. However, the one thing customers *can* agree on today is that the Internet has accelerated their expectations . . . from you.

The On-Demand Customer

The globalization of electronic commerce has provided your customers with unlimited choices as well as the ability to conduct instant side-by-side comparisons.

Nowadays, all customers (both consumer and B2B) are convinced they can get anything *they* want anytime *they* want it at *their* complete convenience. And, quite honestly, they're usually right.

Think about it; your cable or satellite TV service makes it possible for you to watch, pause, rewind, or record a television show to watch later at *your* convenience (even zipping through the commercials, if you like). Amazon's Kindle (just discussed) lets you download the latest best seller from any Wi-Fi connection and begin reading it in minutes. Netflix will stream your favorite movie to your computer or TV almost before you finish reading this paragraph. Facebook allows you to find long-lost friends in an instant; in fact, you can create a network of new and old friends with a few clicks of a mouse. When you sign up for an RSS feed (on virtually any subject that interests you), the very latest information is pushed to you the moment it happens.

Anything and everything is available online. If you want to buy concrete, steel, cattle, rum, or any one of 10,000 vintage Corvette parts, reliable e-commerce sites are ready to take and ship your order 24 hours a day, seven days a week. Your customers can, in essence, make time stand still!

Can you see why this matters to *you?* Your customers are accustomed to being served in real time. Most of their daily activities—from getting drive-through meals to ATM banking, from TV-DVR recording to self-checkout at Home Depot, from digital photography to text messaging, to anything you can think of—allow them to truly manipulate time to suit *their* schedules. On-demand buying is their way of squeezing you into their compacted lives. You can't use the excuse, "That doesn't apply to us because we are not an Internet company."

Please, don't delude yourself. You are being compared to the rest of your customers' worlds, which are ramping up to respond more quickly to their impatience. Frankly, if you don't respond at digital speed, your customers will consider you substandard. If you don't make their time a priority, you could be perceived as arrogant, too old-school, and maybe even lazy.

Smart organizations recognize the importance of a hyper-quick turnaround. We believe so strongly in this trend that our company has retitled our customer service education program Customer Urgency.

I'll Get Back to You within 24 Hours . . . *or Maybe Never*

We know a certain real estate agent who is quite exceptional and whose clients all love him. However, if you call his cell phones, you will probably hear this message: "Hey, I'm glad you called. I'm either on the other line or I'm showing a house. Please leave a detailed message, and I will try to get back to you within 24 hours."

Huh, 24 hours? A few years ago, a message like that might have been acceptable, but not today. A 24-hour response time sounds like *years* to a customer with a problem. The customer saw your website or got a recommendation from a friend—and he or she needs attention *right now*, not 24 hours from now.

As Vancouver, British Columbia–based consultant Mark Smiciklas says, "I am constantly amazed by the fact that some companies don't bother to respond to website information requests . . . acknowledge voice mails . . . reply to e-mails, and so on. It's safe to say that being totally ignored represents the extreme end of the (bad) service spectrum. Few will argue that indifference is not a good customer service strategy. But what constitutes reasonable or excellent service in today's marketplace? When I research a product or service online, I find myself getting agitated if I don't get a reply acknowledging my interest within the same business day."

Do You Respond This Fast?

If you place an online order with Amazon.com, you get an e-mail confirming your order within 30 seconds of placing it. Amazon includes a web link so that you can track your order throughout the process. The minute your order is filled, you get another e-mail advising you that your order has been shipped, along with the tracking number to trace the order if you need to. Now, *that's* respectful and responsive. Even though you haven't even spoken to a human being at Amazon, you feel well served. Amazon treats every order with this kind of urgency, regardless of the size.

When my son, Adam, did the research for my book *The Customer Shouts Back*, here are some of the visceral comments he recorded: "I called twice with my order. The sales rep never got back to me." "The service manager made a promise to solve my problem by tomorrow, but we didn't get our car back for a week." "I was told my problem would be fixed ASAP. To me, ASAP meant a few days. To the company, [it] meant a few months."

ASAP means two different things, indeed.

When I used to ask my youngest son, Ryan, to clean his room, he would come in from playing outside and head to his room—like the wonderfully obedient kid he was. Thirty minutes later, Ryan would walk into the living room and announce, "It's clean, Dad. Now, can I ride my bike?" Knowing that my son was proud of having completed his task, I knew I only had to survey the landscape and officially compliment him. But when I walked into his room, I saw that he had merely shoved his dirty clothes under his bed and thrown his toys into the closet. I remember saying, "This is not what I meant by clean, son."

My idea of clean wasn't Ryan's idea of clean. To paraphrase a line from the Paul Newman movie *Cool Hand Luke,* we clearly had a "failure to communicate."

Customer urgency from the customer's point of view may not be what *you* consider urgent. So, after studying a stack of angry evaluation forms, we thought you might like to hear what your on-demand customers expect from you.

I'm Your 2011 Customer. Please Listen to Me

I work hard, and I'm a busy person. I've had a lot going on in my life before I decided to contact you. I am worried about my home equity and my 401(k). I am worried about keeping my job. I want to get my kids into good schools. My spouse isn't the easiest person to live with. My friends call me several times a day to talk about *their* problems. And I have older relatives who need my attention. Now I have a new problem I think you may be able to solve. I think I need one of your products or one of your services. Here are my expectations:

1. *Immediately acknowledge me when I visit you in person.* Don't keep talking on the phone or texting your friends when I am standing in front of you. If you do that, I will feel unimportant and I will resent giving you my money (if I choose to do so at all).
2. *If I call you on the phone, don't put me on hold for more than one minute without checking back with me.* And don't connect me to a long series of menu

options. Those automated instructions can never understand what I want. Don't let me hear you arguing with a coworker or another customer in the background. If you do, I will feel ignored and probably hang up.

3. *Understand that my time is valuable and that I expect you to help me as quickly as you can.* In fact, my life is so packed with activities and obligations that I usually wait until the last minute to get help. If you don't respect my time, I will feel like you are dismissing or even rejecting me.

4. *If you make a promise to me, I will expect you to keep it.* I always keep my promises, so I expect the same from you. Otherwise, I will think you may be just stalling—or worse, lying to me. If that is the case, I won't trust what you say the next time.

5. *I won't hold any unforeseeable delays against you—as long as you are honest with me about the reason.* Include me in the process so that I know you are working on it. If I find out later that the reason you gave me was a lie, I will never give you my money again.

6. *If I am not satisfied with the outcome, assure me that you will fix it and make me happy.* If we cannot agree on what "happy" is, then at least put yourself in my shoes and do the right thing. Refund my money. Give me a credit toward a future purchase. Offer me a service of equal value. If you can't do any of those, at least apologize for wasting my time. Admit your mistakes and don't blame me for being a high-maintenance customer. After all, when I came to see you, I intended to spend my hard-earned money with *you*, not with your competitors.

On Demand = Real Time

Software solution company ASG recently held a conference at which research company Forrester vice president and principal analyst John Pierre Garbani announced the following statistic: "Ninety percent of IT executives surveyed think that a real-time, customized dashboard will improve service levels and problem remediation. IT executives who implemented this type of dashboard . . . were able to improve IT efficiency, increase end user satisfaction with business services, and reduce outages, thus improving business users' productivity."

How Will You Spot the Next Customer Revolution?

You can actually pinpoint the next customer behavior revolution if you pay attention to significant out-of-our-control social events, peer-to-peer occurrences, and technology waves. These events are so shocking that normal human behavior patterns cannot help but be disrupted and reinvented.

For example, after the September 11, 2001, World Trade Center catastrophe in New York City, millions of people were scared. Formerly confident Americans realized that nobody was safe anymore. We worried about opening our mail, because it could contain anthrax. We couldn't go to shopping malls or amusement parks, because public places like that might be considered high-value targets. Life in America became jarringly fragile and mortal. Our collective consciousness started to agree on one thing: "If my life is snuffed out tomorrow, then I am going to experience as much as I can today." According to our research, this meant that people wanted a memorable experience, whether eating at a restaurant, picking up their clothes from a dry cleaner, exiting a CPA's office, or buying a car from an auto dealer. Every moment had to be emotionally satisfying and memorable. It was as if every American were a death row inmate ordering his or her last meal—every single day.

Social scientists Joe Pine and James Gilmore looked like soothsayers when they wrote *The Experience Economy* in 1999. They made the argument that brands must become more theatrical by creating memorable events for their customers. Disney does it. Las Vegas does it. You can do it, too. The feelings and memories that your experiences provide often *become* the product itself.

No doubt you work in a business culture that demands a great customer experience. In fact, you may have designed metrics to test the consistency of your accomplishments in that area.

After the Experience . . . Came *Empathy*

Our own research conducted in 2006 prompted customers to inform us that escalating housing costs (a factor that is clearly out of our control) required both members of the household to work long hours. Customers were busier than ever just trying to pay their mortgage and SUV payments. And while many still wanted a great experience, they also wanted you to do all of the heavy lifting for them. They simply didn't have time or the expertise. Business consultant David Maister, who coined the phrase "trusted advisor" (and wrote the book on this subject) described the tailor-made solution for this phenomenon. At the core of what *trusted advisor* means in the context of customer service is "empathy." Customers need someone they can trust, someone who understands their fragile emotional states, someone who can hold their hands as they cross into unknown territory. My company even started a Customer Empathy Institute in conjunction with California State University at Monterey Bay to coach leaders on how to behave as trusted advisors—albeit with empathy.

Now, as I've described, technological advances in e-commerce have given rise to the next thing they want: *customer urgency.*

Peer-to-Peer Customer Evolution You *Can* Control

There are two kinds of peer-to-peer customer behavior shifts. The first shift causes behavior against you. The second causes behavior in your favor. Let's take a look at the bad news first.

One customer complains to a friend about a bad situation you somehow created (maybe even inadvertently). The other friend concurs with person number one because he or she has had the same lousy experience. As more friends start agreeing and comparing notes, they decide to do something about it. Their action may be something as simple as spreading the word that Business XYZ is shady and overpriced, which results in everyone agreeing to shop elsewhere. Business XYZ could have prevented the exodus if its practices were clean and aboveboard.

Your argument could be, "Yeah, but I don't want those kinds of customers anyway." Maybe you could afford to be picky 20 years ago. But new-school word of mouth quickly goes viral. It can be as extreme as the overthrowing of a dictatorial Egyptian government by a handful of college students who started complaining on Facebook: One emotional video was posted on Facebook; within a few hours, 60,000 people had seen it and agreed to protest in downtown Cairo. Just 18 days later,

President Hosni Mubarak resigned and left the city. The transformations didn't end with Egypt; now, many Middle East power structures are being challenged by a new power that's being organized by web-based social networking. Didn't see *that* coming, did you?

Before your business is toppled, monitor what is being posted about you on the web by going to www .addictomatic.com. This allows you to read what is being said and where it is being said. You can even find the sources and reply to them. Or you can take countermeasures by entering good news about your company. For example, McDonald's Corporation has a team of people reading every post about McDonald's on Twitter and Facebook. If they read about a person who has had a bad experience, McDonald's will send that person a coupon redeemable at one of its restaurants. If you don't want to monitor your own reputation, there are plenty of reputation management companies that will do it for you.

The other kind of word of mouth is the kind that changes customer behavior in your favor. It's a more traditional way of spreading news—something that existed long before metrics and social networking. Business building goes viral when one person has a great experience and tells a friend . . . who then tells two friends . . . and so on. Before long, that new experience shifts cultural behavior. It can be as simple as getting a good night's sleep.

Branding and Service: The Perfect Storm

Successful market share thieves are able to finesse a high-pressure customer experience into low-pressure customer service to achieve the perfect "brand storm."

Westin Hotels caused such a culture shift by introducing the Heavenly Bed in 1999. It's important to note that even though it had been a successful hotel chain since 1930, Westin didn't think of this idea. Travelers told Westin in a survey that the most important component of staying in a hotel was to get a good night's sleep. Working backward from that sentiment led to the idea of developing a comfier bed. Westin took the idea seriously and installed 52,000 beds in 39,500 guest rooms—an endeavor that cost the company $30 million. The wildly satisfied customers made the Heavenly Bed the new standard, essentially forcing other hotels into providing an equally satisfying experience. Sheraton now features the Sweet Slumber bed, Marriott has the Revive Collection, Disney offers the Resort Bed, Hilton showcases the Serenity Bed, and so on.

The Heavenly Bed not only changed the customer's expectations for a good night's sleep, it also became a wildly popular brand for Westin. To date, Westin has sold more than 32,000 Heavenly Beds at over $3,600 each. It can also sell you other Heavenly-branded products, from candles to dog collars. Strong brands like these are a profit center, not just a gimmick.

Homework

- ◆ What is your usual response time for customer and client requests?
- ◆ Could you improve your on-demand response time? In which areas could you accelerate?
- ◆ Does everyone in your organization have a sense of customer urgency?
- ◆ How important is customer empathy in your organization? What could you do to significantly improve in this area?

- What do your customers keep asking you for that you are currently not giving them? Why not?
- What kind of negative word of mouth do you hear about your organization?
- What can you do to start a positive word-of-mouth revolution? Are you using reputation management tools?
- Could you change the conversation in your industry, as Westin did? If so, what could you do that would make your competitors chase you?

Chapter 4

User-Generated Leadership Rocks!

Dumb Is the New Smart

I was lucky enough to have a few conversations with Johnny Carson, the King of Late Night Television (1962–1992), who used to quip, "I guess I'm smart enough to be dumb." For a man who attracted millions of television viewers every night for *30 years*, Johnny's not-so-tongue-in-cheek advice was to remember that there is no future in trying to outsmart your customers.

We shouldn't attempt to use such an approach, either. We shouldn't insist that we know what our customers want or how they want it. I like Christine Romans' financial philosophy, as conveyed in the title of her book *Smart Is the New Rich*. But for stealing market share, I prefer "Dumb is the new smart."

In 2003, Jim Collins, author of the best-selling *Good to Great*, proclaimed that the most effective leaders in companies are executives who are humble yet ambitious for their companies rather than for themselves. One of the former CEOs whom Collins interviewed for his book was Darwin Smith, former chief executive of paper-product-based manufacturer Kimberly-Clark. Smith, like Johnny Carson, approached his job in the role of a servant who doesn't know all of the answers, admitting, "I never stopped trying to become qualified for the job."

In the even-more-complex world of 2011, humility seems to have gathered steam. Smart "dumb" leaders are increasingly acknowledging what they don't know and depending on the crowd to help them innovate and manage their organizations' futures.

The Crowd Knows

Crowdsourcing is all about accessing the crowd for new information (and innovations) regarding your business. Sounds closely associated with the collective consciousness I keep jamming down your throat, doesn't it? It is, but with a slightly more aggressive bent—on *your* part. If you are already paying attention to where the culture is going, then why not be more proactive? Don't wait for the culture of the crowds to tell you where it's going; boldly ask that very question.

Crowdsourcing is a way for you to connect with the part of the culture that already knows you: your fans. Admit you don't know everything and ask for their help in developing new products or services. They will probably be able to tell you whether you're relevant or not. All you need is a response mechanism—a way for your particular crowd to talk to you. A forum or website is infinitely better than a boilerplate customer-valuation form.

Even if they don't know you (yet), you can entice them to get acquainted. Apple demonstrated the power of crowdsourcing when it opened its source codes—and then paid out $2 billion dollars to ordinary people who could create applications for its iPhones and iPads. But you're not Apple, so maybe you'll be inspired by some other models of listening to (and engaging) the crowd for innovation.

On October 1, 2006, Netflix offered $1 million to the first developer of a video-recommendation algorithm that could beat its existing one. An AT&T research team called BellKor combined with software company Commendo's team BigChaos and others to win the 2009 grand prize of $1 million. Similarly, coffee giant Starbucks uses the website www.mystarbucksidea.com to solicit new innovations and ideas. After 200,000 submissions, one brilliant innovation emerged from the crowd: the splash stick, a little green stopper for cups that keeps coffee from splashing out. See? Even the people who work at Starbucks and know that coffee spills from the tiny little hole on top needed some independent eyes on the problem.

UTest is a network of independent, international testers (aka "the crowd") who can be mobilized to test your web applications, mobile devices, gaming, and desktop solutions. Companies like Google, Microsoft, Intuit, BBC, Groupon, MySpace, Thomson Reuters, and dozens of others hire UTest to improve quality, shorten time-to-market, or to help curb the costs of testing new products. Even corporate giant General Electric is getting involved with this movement by creating its EcoMagination Challenge, an initiative that invites businesses, entrepreneurs, innovators, and students to submit breakthrough ideas for home energy creation, management, and use. That's right, GE offers money in exchange for great ideas from the crowd! GE will award each of five innovation challenge award recipients $100,000 in cash, for a total of $500,000. GE is anxious to promote these entries as examples of outstanding entrepreneurship and innovation.

Dream This!

When it finally welcomes its first commercial passengers on board, the 787 Dreamliner jet will be the undisputed success story of the Boeing fleet. But even Boeing didn't presume that it could build the Dreamliner without help. According to company spokesperson Loretta Gunter, "It would be arrogant to think that all of the best ideas and best technologies exist within the walls of Boeing."

Upon thinking it through, Boeing enlisted the crowd and organized a mass collaboration effort from brands such as Honeywell, Mitsubishi, Kawasaki, General Electric, and 96 of its other suppliers. During the exhaustive design process, engineers from 100 such companies used sophisticated database software. They traded plans, chatted online, accessed each other's designs, and conducted simulations in real time to make sure that no incompatibility problems would surface later.

Keep in mind that many of these companies were intense competitors of Boeing. It would seem that there would be a huge risk that one or more of the companies might restrain themselves from giving up their best stuff. However, Boeing made it clear that if too much innovation were kept under wraps, the consequences would be brutal for the rest of the team.

Did accessing the crowd work? It sure did. Boeing was able to cut a year off the design process, and the 787 Dreamliner has been the fastest-selling airplane in the company's history. So far, Boeing has 843 net orders at $150 million each—not a bad outcome.

User-Generated T-Shirts

Threadless is a famous crowdsourcing success story that actually employed the crowd before crowdsourcing was even a word. This T-shirt company invites artists to upload their artwork to be considered for a Threadless design. The company then displays the artwork on its website, and the Threadless web community (with more than a million web visitors) has a chance to vote on designs they like. Each design is scored, and each week the brand management team at Threadless takes a look at the top-scoring designs and chooses a few to print. What's even cooler for the designers is that winners receive $2,000 in cash, a $500 gift certificate, and $500 every time there is a reprint of that design.

How did Threadless get a community of more than a million visitors? Well, if you're an artist who has submitted your design, you just lobby all of your friends to vote for you. You can see where this is going: T-shirt designs—*American Idol* style.

Threadless has been such a flashpoint for social networking that it has attracted 80,000 artists so far. Add in the friends of these 80,000 designers and the numbers get big, really fast. Cofounder Jake Nickell says that the success of Threadless isn't because it's a great brand; rather, it's due to the fact that Threadless is a strong self-generating community of creativity. Do you see what's happened here? The public consciousness—the community, the fans, the artists, and their friends—has catapulted Threadless into a $30 million, 50-employee company. Threadless will probably never have paid artists on its staff. The company doesn't need to. It has artists on every street corner who are working for a prize worth more than the money: public recognition.

When *Not* to Use the Crowd: Caveat Emptor *Evaluatus*

You can already tell I am a huge fan of the profit potential that can come from mirroring the collective consciousness. Maybe it comes from my father, Chuck Shafer, who once said, "It's always easier to ride a horse in the direction it's going." But there is a vast difference between observing the crowds (and leveraging *their already determined* direction) and *asking* them to help solve your problems for you. Do you trust everything they say? What if their advice is wrong? They can walk away and stop for an ice cream cone, while you have to stay behind and manage the consequences.

If you decide to engage the crowd for innovation (and I clearly think you should), you will still have to exercise careful discernment before blindly trusting their judgment. When you give the crowd an opportunity to brainstorm ideas for what you do, the vast majority of their suggestions will land in the arena of "cool yet impractical." Take note that 200,000 ideas flowed through MyStarbucksIdea.com before the splash stick . . . well, uh . . . *stuck* with the company. And realize that Boeing enlisted 100 engineers for the 787 Dreamliner: 100 top engineers who cross-checked each other's work (and who all had to *agree*) before a significant design change could take hold. Imagine the safety consequences if Boeing had lurched ahead on every cool idea. Would you want to fly on a plane that was built in this way?

In the same vein, Threadless doesn't print *every* design it receives online. Of the thousands submitted, approximately 10 per week are actually printed. Despite its intense reliance on the crowd's involvement, Threadless still has a brand management team that must carefully decide which designs are fit to print—and which will meet the standards their loyal customers expect.

Asking the Crowd for Ideas Is Very Different from Asking Them to Evaluate Your Performance

Customer/client evaluations are always a tricky proposition because you so desperately want validation that you are pleasing the people who pay you money. But if you refer to the preceding argument about *asking* for help from your crowd, you'll be wary when asking them to (1) recall and (2) articulate their experience with you in the words you've constructed in your survey. Because our company has been studying customer behavior since 1994, we have paid particular attention to how the repeat-buying habit indicates loyalty after the survey. I wrote extensively about this in *The Customer Shouts Back* and *Are You Relevant?* To save you time, I'll compress my findings into a single sentence: Customers *hate* evaluating you.

As we discussed in Chapter 3, your customers lead extremely busy lives. They don't have time to fill out your form. Although they can probably remember the feeling they had *after* the transaction, they can't recall the intricacies and details of the experience you're asking them for. Therefore, they don't know how to score you properly.

Remember, this averse reaction to surveys (from our research) refers to a *collective* consciousness. What do *most* people respond to? What basic experiences do most people like or dislike? Surveys fall easily into the "dislike" category.

From my experience in show business, it was a given that the final moment of every performance had to be the most memorable. It was the moment during which the entire audience would gasp, cry, laugh, or be scared . . . to the point of insisting their friends see the show. The barometer we used to judge a performance was the encore. Did enough of the audience love the program so much that they wanted *more*?

In television, the most seductive episode is the cliffhanger. The cliffhanger is a moment that is so compelling and poses so many unanswered questions that you will wait until next year to see what happened. Even the evening news uses the cliffhanger. Think about it: Television news is primarily horrifying. Earthquakes. Murders. Kidnappings. Celebrity arrests. Tornados. Burglary. Your favorite sports team lost. Not a great and wonderful experience. Yet news stations want you to like them enough to tune in tomorrow night. So, at the end of each gory broadcast, they present the reliable kicker story.

The kicker story is the happy ending. No matter how bad the news may be, the newscasters will lighten things up at the very end of the broadcast by showing a video of a parrot teaching a dog to meow, a baby break-dancing, or a 300-pound man jumping into (and collapsing) his aboveground pool. The kicker story is, of course, followed by happy-host chat segment where the broadcasters go off script to ask each other what they will do over the weekend. Incidentally, the strategy works.

Final moments executed (consistently premeditated) in this way cause you to prefer one station over another. Repeat business. Loyalty. Familiarity.

Now that you know the importance of the final moment, how does it apply to the survey?

Let's say you create an awesome experience for your customers. You show empathy, urgency, and kindness. You resolve a problem—and even become genuinely friendly as the transaction closes. Customers leave thinking, "I liked that. I'm going back next time." Even though they may not have the words to describe it, the memory they associate with you feels good. They could say at the end of the transaction that *you* were a good experience.

A week later they get a written survey in the mail or a phone survey inquiry from your organization. Because you are now offering an hors d'oeuvre they didn't order and don't have time to eat, this moment becomes their *new* final moment. You have probably just destroyed all the goodwill you built during the actual transaction. The first thing they do with a written survey is to go to the last page and see how many questions they are supposed to answer. If the process is too daunting, they will throw it away.

Telephone surveys elicit an even worse reaction. Many telephone surveys are timed to be conducted at mealtime hours, because surveyors know that most people are home at this time. However, your targets are trying to settle in for dinner—and you risk driving them away forever because you want "only five minutes" of their private time.

One last caveat before I offer a solution.

When you're developing a survey form, think about the people who have to complete it. Will it be convenient, short, and easy to understand? Or did you design the form so it would easy for *your* team to tabulate the scores? Oh, and did you annoyingly fill it with every possible question you could think of because the boss is pressuring you to find out why your business unit is failing?

If you want accurate feedback, keep the form *very* short, and don't use words and phrases that no human being would use in normal conversation. Let me put this in context for you:

> "Hey, Bob, did Cynthia's pot roast *exceed* or just *meet* your expectations?"
>
> "Danny says Heather is funny, but I *strongly disagree.*"
>
> "Was it a good haircut? I don't know. I am *least likely* to go there again."

Every organization works overtime trying to design the proper methods for measuring customer satisfaction. They call it the *voice of the customer.* Well, if you really want to hear this voice, then consider the following: This book is about growing your organization at a rate above the predicted recovery growth rate. I maintain that you'll accomplish that if you grab business from your lazy competitors. Therefore, what can you ask the customer that would directly stimulate actions dedicated to growth?

Only *One* Question Matters . . . Really

Fred Reichheld, fellow of the management consultancy Bain & Company, figured out that of all the survey questions you can ask a customer, only one really matters: "How likely are you to recommend us to your friends?"

That's it! Reducing your evaluation form to a single question is immutably elegant in its simplicity.

If we want to truly take market share from our competitors (in a 1 percent growth recovery), we need to create such a satisfying and emotional impression with our current customers that they run to their friends and insist they do business with *us*. If you buy Fred's book *The Ultimate Question*, you'll learn how to create a metric he calls "the Net Promoter Score"—a simple 0 to 10 scoring system anyone can understand. You want to know how many people promote you to their friends and associates. You also want to know which customers (and behaviors) detract from spreading the good word about you. Subtract the bad scores (0–8 = detractors) from the good scores (9–10 = promoters) and you end up with a Net Promoter Score.

Seriously, only one question? Okay, if you insist, Reichheld will allow you to add a second (more qualitative) question: "What did we do that caused you to answer the way you did in Question #1?" There, now the customer can tell you in his or her own words what went right or wrong.

I can feel your skepticism through these pages. You would like to take me by my lapels into the boardroom and flog me with every market-researched reason you *must* ask 89 survey questions, right? But corner me and I'm stubborn on this issue. Consider, as well, that companies who are thriving during this recovery—American Express, Charles Schwab, eBay, Microsoft, General Electric, Procter & Gamble, Boeing, Symantec, Verizon Wireless, Intuit, Enterprise Rent-A-Car, HomeBanc, and thousands of others—are all using the Ultimate Question Net Promoter Score system to respectfully learn more about what they are doing to grow (or shrink) their organizations. I'm urging you to explore NPS before your competition catches onto this.

Consider this: What have you got to lose by respecting your customer's time?

Homework

- ◆ How open are you as a leader to hearing new ideas? (Be honest!)
- ◆ Do you ever find yourself acting smug because of your success? If so, do you realize that your attitude will deter you from finding new ideas and new resources?
- ◆ How can you engage the crowd to help you solve a problem or to develop a new product or service?
- ◆ Can you tempt the crowd to pitch in? If so, what monetary or publicity value can you offer them that sounds reasonable to you?
- ◆ Can you collaborate with other like-minded organizations (as Boeing did) to take your industry to a whole new level? If so, which competitors would you consider for collaboration?
- ◆ How complicated and long are your customer/ client/patient evaluation forms? Are they designed for *your* convenience or for that of the person who fills it out?

◆ Why not try experimenting with the Net Promoter Score method described by Fred Reichheld?

◆ What are you doing in the final moment of the transaction to create a positive associative memory with your customers?

Chapter 5

Which Trusted Advisors Will Lead the Recovery?

Most Trusted Advisors Miss the Point

Almost every C-suite executive has read David Maister's book on the subject, aptly titled *The Trusted Advisor*. They have caught the bug and now want the infection to go airborne. This movement is significant, because encouraging all salespeople to become trusted advisors is akin to making the not-so-secret admission that e-mail, voice mail, IM-ing, texting, and most forms of electronic customer relations management (CRM) software just aren't cutting it. Organizations that want to take business away from a competitor are getting back to the face-to-face basics.

I'll start by giving some examples of what a trusted advisor looks like in practice, and then we'll get into the nuts-and-bolts skills and behaviors required to master this art.

Before Ramani Ayer retired as the CEO of The Hartford Insurance Company in 2009, he told me the following: "The future is not electronic. It [requires] getting more feet on the street. I want every agent and associate to stop staring at their CRM dashboards and get out of the office. I want them to spend 65 percent of their time with their customers."

Jon Magnusson, chairman and CEO of renowned Seattle, Washington–based structural and civil engineering firm Magnusson Klemencic Associates, has planned and built some of the most stunning, award-winning projects in the world. MKA's designs include stadiums that hold 72,500 people, 48 museums in 11 states and three countries, urban towers and stacks to 112 stories, luxury hotels, and 40 convention centers totaling 18 million square feet. Suffice it to say that MKA has a stellar reputation. With a matchless track record, you wouldn't expect that this company would have to work *that* hard for business.

But it does.

As Magnusson told me, "We never take our business for granted. We have 7,000 active accounts and we treat everyone like he or she is our best friend. We believe in very long-term relationships. But it doesn't come by accident. People trust us because we work hard to keep our promises, and we do excellent work."

I love to use examples from the commercial building trade, because it was a segment that was hit the hardest in the credit crunch of 2008–2009. So many companies in that space went under, but the solid ones that weathered the storm and kept growth in mind are inspiring.

General contracting company Mortenson Construction received the 2010 Wisconsin Design-Build Project award, a national award conferred by the Design-Build Institute of America (DBIA). It's a bit deceiving, because Mortenson is a $1.2 billion a year company responsible for large building construction all over the planet. President and CEO Tom Gunkel says, "We don't assume our relationships or reputation will win the job. We put our A Team in the presentation. We are 'fee competitive.' We do our homework [each time] like [we're working on] the first bid we've ever done."

The A Team to which Gunkel is referring is made up of the company's top dogs, its most articulate communicators, who can answer every question with confidence and experience. That group represents the trusted advisor concept at the highest-performing level.

What Are the Admired Talents of a Trusted Advisor?

To answer this question with something like "being a good communicator" is too trite and not precise enough for today's demanding customers. Let's be more specific. Is he or she a good storyteller? A witty conversationalist? A good closer? Someone who boasts a photographic memory?

Maybe all of these things, but at the top of the list is this: A communicator *knows when to shut up.*

Sadly, nobody shuts up anymore. Everyone talks without stopping to listen. I'd like to target the social networking phenomenon for encouraging our overdeveloped sense of self-importance.

Free Agent Nation author Daniel Pink estimates that 30 million to 40 million Americans can now work out of their homes with a broadband connection. While it is, of course, nice to be home, the downside is that all of these people are physically isolated from their former coworkers. Communication is done via e-mail, text messaging, and the occasional phone call. "Talking," "collaborating," and "negotiating" aren't skills you get to practice every day. And since these home-based workers *are* human beings and thus need feedback from other human beings, they join various social networking sites (Facebook, Twitter, MySpace, Match.com) in order to stay connected, to be validated, to attract and add other web-hungry isolated individuals—most of whom they never meet.

I have a Facebook page, but I am admittedly not very active. One day last month I decided to stay online for several hours to see what might happen. I noticed that many of my "friends" stay online for hours. They post their thoughts and comments several times a day. If there are 500 million members on Facebook alone, e-chatting with each other, looking for online validation, then there is a serious risk to your self-esteem.

Have You Had This Facebook Conversation . . . with Yourself?

I just posted my most recent random pictures as if to say, "Here is what I like to do and whom I like to do it with."

I post short videos I have recently seen (or uploaded from my phone) to show the world. The inference is, "This is me doing something you may be interested in—but probably not."

I look up people I used to know to see if I can "friend" them.

I look up famous people and take a chance that they will be my "friend." Some accept me. Others don't. I feel rejected. But then I remember that I don't accept everyone, either.

I get invited to join obscure groups or engage in discussions with people who are interested in something I don't think is very cool.

The "What's on your mind?" comment box beckons me. To be funny I write, "I wonder how many people in Burundi have Justin Bieber on their iPods?" But I get offended if nobody reads it—or even replies with a countercomment. In fact, nobody even checked the box, "Like This." I feel stupid. Dejected, I tweet the 38 people who follow me, "I think I will have some egg salad to cheer myself up."

For all of their admittedly fascinating and helpful services, Facebook and Twitter are inadvertently designed to reward virtual self-centeredness—a trend that naturally carries over into real life. It doesn't take long for an expert Facebook subscriber to honestly believe that the world can't wait to see what happens to him or her next.

Seriously, are you really that important? If you think you are, then you're probably not a very good candidate for the role of trusted advisor.

A Lesson from the Talk Show World

During my time as a network talk show and game show host, it was my job to (attempt to) create instant rapport with my guests. If I was going to get the answers to my sometimes sensitive questions, I would have to first establish some trust with that guest.

When you first get a job as a talk show host, you usually get some professional coaching on how to ask questions. The guests were often famous yet skittish celebrities I had never met. The skill I was formally taught—one that most sales professionals and customer service advocates do *not* learn—was to hone the art of intentional curiosity.

It is the talk show host's job to ask *all* of the questions. We drive the interviews, and at no time do we allow the guests to ask us any questions. It's not about the host; it is 100 percent about the guest. I'm a naturally curious dude; but even so, there was a producer, standing behind every guest's head, holding a card with 10 more questions for me to ask. It is a guaranteed way to ensure that a talk show host never runs out of questions.

Johnny Carson once said something absolutely profound—not only for talk show hosts, but for anyone in the sales or relationship professions. I asked him, "John, what qualities do you think you had that kept the public tuned in to you for 30 years?" He said, "Well, there were funnier comedians . . . and you know we didn't always get the hottest guests . . . but the one thing I always tried to keep in mind was [that] I never wanted to be the best guest on my own show."

I truly believe that all trusted advisors should commission the mounting of a large office plaque with this saying for all to see. If a plaque doesn't go with your decor, consider carving Johnny's credo into all of your employees' desks.

Avoid being the best guest on your own show— because if you try to outshine everyone, your customers will lose interest and tune you out. Don't show *mild* interest in the guest; show *extreme* interest. Make it *all about* him or her—because, really, it is. Or at least it should be.

The False Start to a Conversation

Another nugget I mined from the television business was the following: Don't immediately launch into your interview questions when you first meet your guests. Begin with a polite greeting, something simple, such as "Hello, how are you?" I would also try to make a flattering remark about their clothing or accessories, compliment them on a recent statement in the press, or something similar. I would always exercise some kind of short verbal handshake before asking the first *real* question. Why? Because talk show interviews are awkward and stressful. Guests are forced to make a myriad of decisions before they ever arrive at the TV studio: what to wear, how they will answer questions, and which specialized makeup to use to cover a pimple. Slowing things down, being easy to talk to, and being as relaxed as possible is the connective tissue I need to create quick rapport.

RAPPORT KILLER

Salespeople make a deadly mistake if they immediately start a big appointment (either face-to-face or by phone) with a comment like "I know you're a busy person. Let me show you what solutions I have for you today." That approach is rude. It's you doing the talking without questioning the customers about themselves. It's ignoring the fact that you need to establish some level of rapport.

JACK GETS IT

I have a friend named Jack who sells automotive additives. In fact, he sells more additives than anybody else in his company. When Jack walks into a client's office, he quickly looks around for pictures, awards, sports collectibles, out-of-context objects, and so forth. Jack is on the hunt for some connective tissue he can use for the "false start."

One time, Jack inherited a client nobody wanted. The guy was gruff, difficult, and never bought any additives. Jack got the appointment, but before he could sit down, the client barked, "What are you gonna try to sell me today?" Jack smiled and said, "I'd be happy to tell you; but first you have to tell *me* what you're doing sitting on the business end of a Brahma bull?"

Riding a bull must be one of the most dangerous activities a person can do, and this guy had a picture of himself doing it. They talked about bull riding, calf roping, and the kind of boot heels you need to wear when you mount a wild bronco. Jack kept smiling and asking more questions. After 30 minutes, Jack looked down at his watch and said, "Whoa, I've taken more time than you have. If it's all right, I'd like to come back next week sometime." The gruff guy said, "Naw, I wasn't going anywhere for lunch anyways. Show me what you got."

Jack left with a $1,200 order . . . and a solid new account. Now, the gruff guy calls Jack for advice on vintage cars, fishing tackle, pizza places . . . and sometimes even engine additives.

Award Winners Know This

Because I get invited to speak at so many corporate meetings, I usually stay around for the awards presentations. These awards are typically given to the "Salesperson" of or "Customer Advocate" of the year—and I am always very curious to see who will get them. I want to know what talents or skills or connections *that* person has that the other 300 don't.

Here's what I see.

When the emcee announces the winner, that person usually ambles to the podium in a very humble (almost shy) way. If he or she gets a chance to talk into the microphone, the speech is invariably something like this: "Oh my gosh, thank you so much. I want to thank my team . . . and my customers . . . and the talented people who support me. I just never thought it was possible to win this award six years in a row."

Six years in a row?!

That's right. You've seen it, too. Often, the big winner this year has been the winner many times before. What are those winners doing right—again and again and again?

I then make my way backstage where my goal is to chat it up with the winner. Maybe I'll unearth his or her secret formula for being so consistently successful.

Stand by for the revelation.

Every time—and I mean *every* time—I try to learn more about the award winner, within, I'd say, 30 to 40 seconds, I realize that *I'm* the one being interviewed! These winners have the unique ability to deflect questions about themselves and turn every conversation back to whomever they are talking to. Sales and customer service award winners are either naturally curious or have trained themselves to be interested in other people, all for profits' sake. Regardless, the result is consistently predictable.

These encounters stand out so clearly in my mind because most people you meet these days are conditioned to talk about *themselves*. So when someone shows interest in you, it's as if they are injecting you with an addictive drug. You can't get enough of it. You want to be around them more because *they* are so interesting. And what makes *them* interesting is that they want to talk about *you!*

Customers interpret this kind of attention as *caring.* They want to be your friend. With regard to growing your market share, they would much prefer to give their money to you than to your self-absorbed competitor.

My friend Pete Winemiller, senior vice president of Guest Relations for the Oklahoma City Thunder NBA team, puts it this way: "We create better relationships when to listen to learn something rather than when we listen to *respond.*"

Pete's right. Are you the kind of person who listens to a conversation to learn something? Or are you the kind of person who listens *only* to find moments when you can talk about yourself?

Take the following 20-second test. Which scenario best describes your listening style?

Scenario #1

Friend: We just got back from an incredible honeymoon in Paris.

You: Oh, I love Paris. I always buy a new pair of shoes at Charles Jourdan on the Champs-Élysées. Expensive; but when you get back home nobody else will have them.

Scenario #2

Friend: We just got back from an incredible honeymoon in Paris.

You: Really? I want to hear all about it. Where did you stay? Where did you eat? Did you buy anything? What was the weather like?

You Can Learn Intentional Curiosity

Becoming intentionally curious will take some getting used to. But once you try it—and make it a habit—you'll watch your personal and professional life vastly improve. You'll wrangle market share from your competitors, and you'll also win "market share" from your friendships.

If you ever hear yourself blathering on about yourself, shut up.

Homework

◆ Do you clarify the specific behaviors you expect from the trusted advisors in your organization?

◆ Are you naturally curious about other people, or are you mostly curious about yourself?

◆ What can you do to encourage your team to show extreme interest in your customers, guests, clients, or patients?

◆ Do you engage people with the "false start" to make a connection? Or do you immediately launch into your sales pitch because you think you are respecting their time?

◆ Can you get the superstars on your team to teach other team members these skills?

Chapter 6

Not All Contrarian Thinkers Are Crazy

*Conventional Wisdom Dies in
an Unconventional Economy*

When an economy takes a nosedive, a great many intelligent people (and organizations) slip into a frozen state of denial. While the quarterly reports clearly indicate a steady decline in revenue and/or market share, many of the leaders can't believe it's real.

"Something is wrong." Someone suggests, "Let's study this."

"Maybe it has nothing to do with us?"

"Right, it is probably an overall market malaise."

A few organizations change. Others panic. Most do nothing. It's as if the leaders are thinking, "We've weathered storms before. Let's wait it out." Can't you imagine them trying to convince their board of directors (and themselves) by making statements like "We always snap back" or "We've come too far to fail now"?

When you think about organizations like Xerox, General Motors, Kodak, Polaroid, and Blockbuster, which went from market share bulls to hibernating bears, you can imagine how impossible it must have been for them to believe the good old days were truly gone. But, sadly, they were. On the other hand, smaller, more nimble organizations—those that don't have the war chests to wait it out—see the downward trend and immediately take action. Instead of waiting, they decide to aggressively explore the unconventional approaches. They scour the market for opportunities—often opportunities that their competition is too scared to consider.

GroundLink Is a Market Reactive Company

Founded in 2004 by Alex Machinsky, GroundLink is a global provider of transportation services. It operates in 172 countries, where it has revolutionized the taxi, limo, and airport shuttle car service market by using software to aggregate, manage, and provide availability to a network of 45,000 suppliers. It's an incredible accomplishment to be serving 5,000 airports through exclusive partnerships with companies like JetBlue, Royal Caribbean, and Amadeus.

GroundLink's obsession with customer care produced growth rates of 50 percent, year after year. The company was so hot, in fact, that it raised $20 million to expand and keep up with its almost $30 million in revenue.

Then, in 2008, the recession knocked corporate travel to its knees, causing GroundLink to immediately see a 25 percent decrease in revenue, a virtual free fall. Okay, this is a test: What do you do if you're GroundLink?

Whatever you came up with as a solution, I'd bet you didn't guess, "Take inspiration from the Jim Carrey movie *Yes Man*."

Yet the GroundLink solution was to *always* say, "Yes!"

After exhaustive brainstorming by the management team, everyone agreed that saying yes was radical, but certainly not passive. The Yes Campaign, simply stated, was: "We will say yes to anything the customer asks for." If the customer wanted a discount, GroundLink's sales reps said *yes*. If the customer wanted an upgrade, they said *yes*. If the customer wanted something special (no matter how bizarre), they said *yes*.

Furthermore, GroundLink didn't wait for the customer to ask. The folks at GroundLink started posing questions like "What can we do that would be special for you?" "How can we improve your trip?" The customer response was almost immediate. Within 60 days, the company had gone from a 50 percent decrease in revenue to a 25 percent increase in revenue.

Now that the recession is in the recovery phase, GroundLink doesn't have to offer the deep discounts of 2008, but the company learned which kinds of over-the-top services created loyalty in bad times and good.

Body Shops Are Like Wedding Planners

It is hard for me think of a more male dominated business than the automotive body industry. You've all seen reality TV shows like *Pimp My Ride*, *American Body Shop*, *Orange County Choppers*, and so on. These men are tough, smart guys who know how to create dream cars and motorcycles by reshaping iron and painting museum-quality artwork on metal and fiberglass.

So what could they possibly learn from a wedding planner? Enough to revolutionize their industry.

PPG industries make OEM (original equipment manufacturer) automotive finishes for these gifted artists. If you have ever taken your damaged car to a body shop, you automatically take it for granted that the newly repaired section of your car will match the paint on the rest of the car. Companies like PPG hire expert colorists from all over the world to make sure your paint matches; regardless of how old or new the car.

But, as you can probably guess, automotive paints must evolve and innovate in order to stay relevant. PPG is a major force in this field, constantly trying to maintain a superior position in the paint world. For example, PPG wanted to create a "greener" product that also had state-of-the-art performance qualities, so they invented a new line of water-based paint products. To give you an idea of the complexity of this innovation, PPG's Enviro-Prime 2000 lead-free electrocoat contributes to increased vehicle life spans without environmental concerns. Topcoat products like EnviroBase waterborne basecoat and Enviracryl Powder Clearcoat give "green products" a hearty new image at a highly competitive cost. And CeramiClear clearcoat has raised the bar when it comes to scratch resistance, impact mars, and acid etch. On top of the science, waterborne paints provide an even better color match to the manufacturer original color.

And you thought it was just paint?

The problem with introducing a new waterborne paint product was this. Body shops have been using oil-based paints since the 1900s. Painting with oil is a very different process from painting with water. So if PPG wanted a body shop to start using these complex, much improved paint finishes, body shops had to change some very ingrained old habits. PPG had to come to a body shop with a simple step-by-step implementation plan. PPG had to address body shop questions like "If I'm going to retrain my painters, what do I do nine months before we do the changeover?" "How about six months out?" "What do they need to know a week before we make the shift?"

Luckily for PPG management, a woman named Cristina Fronzaglia, who worked in the head office, had been to three weddings in one year. She intuitively applied what every bride must face to the PPG retraining issue.

Every bride knows there is a comprehensive wedding-planning checklist. Most of us men (and probably those of you who are paint engineers and body shop managers) don't know anything about wedding checklists. So for the uneducated, the wedding checklist has a chart that shows what to do one year before the wedding, nine months from the wedding date, three months out, and what to do during the actual wedding ceremony. It's an airtight planner designed to make certain nothing falls through the cracks.

Cristina suggested that PPG adapt such a "planner" to the waterborne paint launch. Genius! PPG took a common idea from the wedding industry and revolutionized the paint training business.

Guess what, their competitors are now introducing their own water-based paints . . . and they are trying to copy the PPG body shop retraining models. But they are probably too late. Body shops have already been training for a year with PPG.

The Flight to Quality

Many of us watched the congressional hearings in December 2008, when the leaders of General Motors, Chrysler, and Ford Motor Company asked for federal bailout money to save their companies. The nation's collective jaw dropped when we heard that the auto executives flew to the meeting in private jets. GM and Chrysler took their licks and took the money.

Ford, however, didn't take the bailout money. Even more impressively, it didn't file for bankruptcy. Instead, Ford did something very American. It rallied from defeat. In fact, Ford knew what was wrong long before Congress called the company on the carpet for accumulating billions in debt (for not being competitive). I attended a Ford conference where executives discussed their staggering losses, which were nearly $3 billion in the third quarter of 2008. I heard the murmurings in the hallways:

Ford executive #1: This is sickening. We have got to cut costs to the bone.

Ford executive #2: Cutting costs is great. But we've got to make cars people want to drive.

In October 2006, a year before the worldwide credit crunch, and a year before the official start date of the recession (December 2007) of the recession, Ford mortgaged the company and raised $23 billion for operating costs. The company then set about building cars that people wanted to drive. In the period between January and June 2010, Ford's profits had grown to $4.7 billion. In fact, sales were up a whopping 15 percent in 2010 over 2009. With its biggest nightmare now in the proverbial rearview mirror, Ford expects to have a positive cash flow by the end of 2011.

How did Ford pull this off? What happened? Did the company capitalize on the lower-priced, fuel-efficient cars people could afford during a recession?

Nope. Exactly the opposite.

Ford knew the recession brought with it a flight to quality. Consumers—the collective consciousness—had a limited amount of money to spend; that much is true. But during the good times, consumers had become accustomed to luxury. They might not be able to afford a Mercedes or BMW; however, they still wanted a stylish, comfortable car that would last a long time. By revamping the Fusion and Taurus with features like heated leather seats, navigation systems, and voice-activated electronics, Ford was able to offer pricier cars (in the $30,000-plus range) and steal market share from the $60,000 market.

You see, you can't force the herd to buy what you sell. You can just do your best to sell them what they want . . . and, of course, still make a profit for yourself.

Motel 6 or Ritz-Carlton?

The hotel industry really took its lumps during the recession. Consumers canceled vacations. They saved money instead of taking a weekend trip to see Grandma. Luxury business travel fell off a cliff when President Obama chastised corporations for extravagant "resort meeting spending" during tough times. The travel industry had a name for the drop-off in hotel and airline spending: the AIG effect.

The *AIG effect* refers to the troubled giant insurance carrier that, on learning in September 2008 that the Federal Reserve would give it an $85 million rescue bailout, had a subsidiary spend $443,000 to entertain independent insurance agents at the five-star St. Regis Resort Monarch Beach in Dana Point, California. The total bailout would reach $173 million. What made the headlines even worse was the fact that AIG awarded additional executive bonuses of $165 million.

The AIG effect virtually crippled the hotel and airline business. As the U.S. Travel Association made clear to the mainstream press: "Business meetings and events account for 15 percent of domestic travel and provide jobs for 1 million people." Nearly every corporate meeting planner was instructed to hold meetings at non-luxury hotels. Even if a company had the money, planners opted for in-house or Skype-type virtual alternatives for the sake of appearances—just to calm the public outcry.

Sadly, there were high-quality casualties. The Five Diamond Ritz-Carlton in Las Vegas had to close its doors in May 2010. Ritz-Carlton spokesperson Vivian Deuschi said, "It's nothing the hotel did. It's a simple lack of business and a decline in the tourism industry." For a tourism industry that took a devastating 15 percent hit due to the firestorm started by AIG, this should never have happened to such a fine property.

But as the economy started coming out of its coma in 2010, business travel began to shed the AIG effect, and professional meetings started to fill hotel rooms again.

Airline flights went from half full to *oversold*. And what's even more interesting is that the hotel rooms weren't "low-end economy." Luxury and ultraluxury hotels got much busier. Demand was coming back—and so were the dollars.

Demand Is Coming Back . . . and Inflation Is Tagging Along

I attended a three-day conference for a high-end hotel chain in early 2011. More than 1,000 hotel general managers were in the room as their chief executive officer laid out the company's five-year plan for growth. Without hedging, he proclaimed, "Demand is coming back stronger than we imagined, so we are committing to build 1,500 hotels over the next five years. Seventy percent of those hotels will be in the luxury category, because [people want] quality. And while our competitors may still try to discount room rates to get our business, we should to be willing to lose a few of those. We do not need to discount any longer. During the recovery we are not going to leave money on the table. Now is the time to take a stand for the luxury brand we offer. Now is the time to be profitable."

This is an inspiring example of each industry being responsible for recognizing demand—and creating its own recovery.

Ultraluxury: Why Aren't You In It?

From cars to hotels, ultraluxury is the new normal for many.

If I were running the upscale department store chain Neiman Marcus, I would tell people, "We own this recovery!" In the third quarter of 2011, Neiman Marcus announced that their profits nearly tripled compared to profits during this time in 2010. If you know this chain, you know that even upscale folks consider Neiman Marcus a luxury to ultraluxury department store. Frankly, they never succumbed to cheapening their brand or brand promise. They know that quality sells even better in a recovery. As a 104-year-old company their confident quality course is time-tested.

CEO Karen Katz says they owe their most recent growth to their genuine passion for customer service and their aggressive online store. Katz insisted on tackling the digital shopping experience by creating not just one but *three* iPad shopping apps. In Katz's words, "We have seen a staggering amount of business coming from people using their iPads."

As you know, this book is about outperforming your lazy competitors, which seems to be a Katzian mantra. Katz is ever vigilant about the activities of her competitors—but not the big stores. Since Neiman Marcus is a strong, reliable brand, worthy of commanding respect from other large retailers, Katz isn't worried about them. Instead, she is wary of the eager start-ups like Moda Operandi and Gilt Groupe. Those smaller forward-thinking companies are nimble enough to tweak their business models overnight.

Katz has the same open-minded approach when it comes to deciding which new brand names penetrate the shelves of her stores. According to Katz, "On any given week, I get about five young entrepreneurs that have a product they think would sell at Neiman Marcus, and we try to be very open because you never know when what they are bringing you could be the next Gucci or the next Prada."

If you're big, it's wise to be a little bit skittish of the smart little guys.

The Six Dollar Burger is Probably Too Cheap

I have been a fan of Carl's Jr. and Hardee's restaurants for a long time. If I had to boil it down, it would have to be the food. It's darn tasty. Their six-dollar burger is worth seven bucks easy. The hamburgers are big and gooey. You've seen their ads. Celebrities like Paris Hilton devouring a burger while decorating her body over a sudsy Bentley. Sweaty Top Chef host Padma Lakshmi nearly makes out with her hamburger while hiking up her skirt on the steps of a stoop (is that possible?). But the topper was Kim Kardashian eating a messy salad in bed; only to take it into the tub for a bubble bath.

If you think I've gotten away from the point you're wrong. Charles Karcher Enterprises (CKE) who owns both Carl's Jr. and Hardees, knows exactly who buys their upscale hamburgers. The bulk of their customers are young men between the ages of 16 and 24.

And you should see CKE's revenue charts. Most analysts agree that the recession started in December 2007. But if you look at the profit charts of Carl's Jr. and Hardees from December 2007 to today (and I have), you see a nice, steady rise. No dip. No free fall. No reason to think this restaurant was off track. Interestingly, during the recession CKE didn't panic themselves into "2 for the price of 1" deals, "value meals," or even "extra value meals." CKE stuck to their big, tasty, gooey burgers, and we were happy to buy in.

While McDonald's, Burger King, and Wendy's battled for the low price family meal buyer, CKE retained high quality and weren't ashamed to charge three to four times the price of their competitors.

And they kept innovating! Carl's Jr. was one of the first burger chains to respond to the low-carb diet craze by offering a big ol' gooey six-dollar hamburger wrapped in a lettuce "bun." And when the low-carb craze died down, the product still sold well to people who suffer from celiac disease, whose diet is restricted by their gluten (wheat) intolerance.

The next innovation happened in 2011 when Carl's Jr. introduced the Charbroiled Turkey Burger. (It also comes in Teriyaki and Guacamole versions.) C'mon now, we've all tasted turkey burgers. They are healthy and lower in calories. So why didn't anyone in the fast food business cash in on them? Because making a turkey burger taste good and still be under 500 calories is an expensive proposition. This was a brilliant move by CKE because an expensive new burger falls right into their sweet spot. How did they get it to taste good and not like day-old meatloaf? The charbroiled turkey burgers at Carl's Jr. and Hardee's were co-developed with *Men's Health's Eat This, Not That* co-author Matt Goulding.

I've been around marketing long enough to know that you can't buy that kind of endorsement. What was so cool about getting a guy like Matt Goulding to participate in designing a new healthy burger is that the folks at CKE hired the artist and didn't tell him how to paint the canvas.

A *Men's Health* thumbs-up satisfies the elite foodies who respect CKE for promoting a healthy diet. But let's talk about store growth. And what about the young male customers who expect some sex appeal in the TV commercials? CKE didn't disappoint. They hired the real Miss Turkey—from the 2010 Miss Universe Pageant. Then, they had her stroll through a huge, gorgeous swimming pool lounge area in high heels and bikini. The fabric pattern on the bikini contained 500 tiny pictures of the Charbroiled Turkey Burger. (Go to YouTube and type in

"Miss Turkey—Charbroiled Turkey Burger" and you'll see the ad.) Even the most ardent "women against men who think women are sex objects" will find it funny.

So successful was the campaign that Carl's Jr. decided to auction off a replica of the Turkey Burger bikini on Ebay. The ending bid was $2,550. The sale of the bikini will benefit Stars for Troops, a new charity program by the fast food company that assists military families and veterans.

Quality Socks Rock

Cabot Hosiery Mills, located in Northfield, Vermont, overcame its own unique challenge during the recession: a sock crisis. For 30 years, Cabot Hosiery had been a wholesale sock manufacturer providing private label athletic socks to retail chain stores like L.L. Bean, Bass, and Orvis, as well as to many of the big-box retailers. But in 2008, the economic slowdown meant deep cuts in every market, including the athletic socks niche.

However, to its great credit, Cabot was prepared. In the early 2000s, the company had made a survival move that would prove invaluable during the recession.

Rather than staying in the shadow of the private label lane, company CEO Ric Cabot and his team created a high-quality brand of their own, called "Darn Tough Vermont," which were knit from 100 percent merino wool, Lycra, nylon, and elastic. Cabot says that the cushioning and material make these socks a perfect solution for skiers, snowboarders, bikers, hikers, hunters, runners, and everyone who wants a light, comfortable, warm, sock that wicks away moisture and wears like iron. Want even more from your sock? Okay, Darn Tough Vermont socks also come with a lifetime, money-back guarantee. Cabot says the fan mail has been staggering: "People say they've tried good socks before, but these are at a different level."

As the world was trying to cut back and save money, third-generation sock man Cabot stuck to a contrarian approach. His opinion was that quality mattered even *more* in tough times. If you have a limited amount of money to spend on socks (or cars or hotels or what have you) then, by golly, you want them to *last.* Cabot is proud of his Made in America heritage, saying, "Nobody ever outsourced anything for quality. We stand by everything we make and if a customer is ever dissatisfied, they can find me here at the mill in Northfield, Vermont. Not many companies can say that."

In tough times, Cabot opted for a flight to quality. According to Mark Cabot (Ric's dad), "We researched the marketplace and found what it needs. There was nobody with a premium performance sock. We focused on a better sock, and it's been extremely successful." Indeed, Darn Tough Vermont is now the number two selling brand in the outdoor specialty market.

Buy Your Competition at Garage Sale Prices

It is contrarian thinking to spend hard-won money (i.e., to expand) during an economic downturn. But spending money the right way can sometimes be your best source for growth. Organizations that hoard their cash and play it safe during a recovery are, in my opinion, wasting a good recession—especially when there are so many underpriced bargains to be had.

Want to grow your market share? Sometimes the answer is to simply buy your competition . . . *on sale.*

I have always loved this quote from Baron Rothschild (of the Rothschild banking family): "The time to buy is when there is blood in the streets." New York mayor and famed financier Michael Bloomberg puts it this way: "I always try to look ahead and avoid the rearview mirror."

My history buff friend (turned stock broker), Jeff Mash, reminded me of this Benjamin Franklin quote: "Buy low. Sell High. I know of no more reliable path to profit."

Now is probably the time for you to buy rather than hoard. Consider the Boston Consulting Group's 1985–2000 recession studies, which stated that "average mergers in a downturn created an 8.3 percent rise in shareholder value after two years, while the average merger in *good times* dropped 6.2 percent within the two years following."

A McGraw-Hill Research study of the 1980–1985 recession came to a similar conclusion: "[The] 600 companies who increased *advertising* expenditures during the 1981–1982 recession significantly experienced higher sales growth, both during the recession *and for three years following.* Those companies rose 265 percent over those that didn't keep up their advertising."

Do you think it can't happen in your industry? Take a peek at the diverse examples that follow.

BANK BARGAINS

Wells Fargo drooled at the bargain it saw. In the midst of the recession, Wells Fargo bought the best of Wachovia Bank for a paltry $45 billion, and its profits in 2009 surged 362 percent. Earnings bounced over $12 billion, making Wells Fargo CEO John Stumpf America's highest-paid banker ($21 million in his total compensation package in 2009).

In Canada, the lending laws still require home buyers to put a substantial amount of their own money down on a house—and to verify they have the income to afford the mortgage payment. (Novel approach, isn't it?) Because of these controls, Toronto Dominion Bank sidestepped the toxic subprime mortgage market and has since gobbled up 1,000 bank branches from Maine to Florida. Toronto Dominion is anxious to get your business. It is open 7 days a week, 361 days a year, and is eager to sell you a mortgage.

RETAIL DOMINATION

Consider, as well, the case of Toys "R" Us. It was already a global retail toy giant when the recession made the brand even more aggressive. Much like Best Buy's customer obsession short-circuited Circuit City, Toys "R" Us targeted competitor KB Toys for extinction—and pulled it off. By 2008, KB shut down 461 stores, leaving Toys "R" Us the undisputed leader in its category, with $13 billion in worldwide sales.

But Toys "R" Us didn't stop there. Determined to gain world retail toy domination, the company bought FAO Schwartz to acquire a premium brand, and it also purchased eToys in order to establish a stronger Internet presence.

BETTING ON PROFESSIONAL ATHLETICS

In the major league sports arena, ESPN has to be applauded for paying attention to the public consciousness and for spending money before reaping the rewards. In 2005, ESPN spent $100 million for the FIFA World Cup soccer TV rights. It predicted that the massive millennial audience who grew up playing soccer would be eager to tune in to the games, and the network also paid attention to the growing Latino population in America. ESPN's bet paid off, as its viewership of World Cup soccer doubled between 2006 and 2010.

THE NEXT ENERGY

Of course, I cannot leave out an energy company that took advantage of recession-induced deals. In April 2009,

Valero Energy, oil refiners and operators of Valero and Diamond Shamrock gas stations, bid on seven bankrupt ethanol plants owned by VeraSun (the nation's second-largest ethanol producer). While the price tag of $447 million may seem like a lot of cash, Valero paid only 30 cents on the dollar.

It won't take long for Valero to start getting a fat return on its investment. Congress has mandated doubling the use of corn ethanol to 15 billion gallons by 2015.

The lesson here is simple: Bad timing for some companies can sometimes mean stunning profits for others.

An Automaker Outfoxes Itself

General Motors was a true contrarian thinker when it produced the EV1 electric car from 1996 through 1999. No other automaker went after this market with such zeal. However, GM discontinued production in 2002.

With energy and environmental concerns gaining in popularity since 2002, my longtime friend Bill Nye (of *Bill Nye the Science Guy* fame) tells me that General Motors picked the exact wrong time in history to stop producing the electric car. Bill drove (and enjoyed) the car for two years until GM wanted it back. While some fans believe General Motors stopped production because maintaining a parts inventory would be cost-prohibitive, GM claims that only 800 units were leased, which clearly did not generate enough income, considering that GM had invested $1 billion in the project.

Much like Kodak, which had invented digital photography and then watched its competitors bask in the market share victories, GM has had to sit back and watch Honda sell 610,000 hybrids worldwide. GM is probably even angrier to see Toyota gloat over the 690,000 units it sold last year.

If you have the nerve to be a contrarian, then stand tall and have the courage of your convictions. It's the curse—and glory—of all forward-thinking contrarians.

Homework

◆ Brainstorm ideas that are totally opposite of conventional wisdom. What are the reasons you're not experimenting with a new twist?

◆ How would focusing on quality over lowest price change your business model?

◆ How would your competitors react to such a shift in your business model?

◆ Inflation is coming, and the cost of operating at a profit will change. Devise a price or fee structure that *doesn't* include discounting.

◆ Have you explored other organizations that could be purchased (by you) at a ridiculous bargain? If it is a business that would expand your market or complement your operations, what is stopping you from making a low bid for the company?

◆ Have you cut back on advertising, marketing, and hiring to save money? Have you considered pouring money back into those areas, given the high potential postrecession upside?

Chapter 7

To Office or Not to Office

Your Future Workforce Doesn't Want One

"What does the public consciousness want?" When you stew about this question, don't restrict your thinking to how (and why) they spend their money within your industry. You also have to consider how *they* want to come to work for you. I'll never forget a conversation I had with some code writers at computer chip maker Intel. The engineers were vocal about how much they loved the company—as well as the caché that goes with getting a paycheck from such an internationally known brand. I asked them if there was anything they *didn't* like about Intel. One young programmer didn't even hesitate: "Yeah, the only thing that bugs me is that fact that they make us come to the office." Because these programmers can do their jobs from a closet in their parents' home, they don't understand why they have to log in at a workplace.

You already know that many people can work from home and that many of them love it. With a good broadband connection, they can work from Starbucks, Barnes & Noble, or Waikiki Beach, for that matter. And some do!

But that's only what's happening above the waterline. What lies beneath?

There is a movement afoot for which you—and many other professionals—might not be prepared. I'm talking about the distinct possibility that the majority of your workforce could work from a remote location. It's called Results Only Work Environment (ROWE), which, simply stated, is a leadership attitude that says, "I don't care where you work as long as you get the result we need."

ROWE, which is being rapidly adopted, is an employment model first articulated and executed by Cali Ressler and Jody Thompson, two former Best Buy employees. These two women convinced management that *results* were the only metric that mattered. It began with the success of a few small test groups; today, 4,000 Best Buy corporate employees have no schedules, no mandatory meetings, and no "keeping busy to impress management" posturing. According to Diana Gray of Oracle Financial Strategies, "Best Buy has seen productivity increase 35 percent. Decreases in turnover rates are 90 percent in some divisions—saving $13 million per year in reduced turnover replacement costs alone."

Ressler and Thompson chronicled their adventures in their book, *Why Work Sucks and How to Fix It*, and it didn't take long for other organizations to see the benefits.

Gap Outlet president Art Peck says, "ROWE works for us because 76 percent of our workforce has an average age of 34. We are in one of the worst commute cities and most expensive places to live [San Francisco]."

What kinds of jobs qualify for off-site work? ROWE applies to Gap executives in merchandising, design, production, finance, human resources, and information technology (IT). When you allow smart, responsible people to work wherever they want, the results can be very impressive. Excuse me, you're probably hung up on the "responsible" part of that last sentence. You might worry that ROWE allows a venue for slackers to apply greater slackness, or perhaps you think that ROWE sounds too risky. Are you a leader who believes in crack-the-whip supervision because you think employees would abuse the privilege of working off-site? First of all, you do realize that you should only be *hiring* responsible people, right? And second, results are the metric for success. If someone slacks, the work will suffer—and you'll let that person go.

Maybe the numbers will persuade you. Here's what happened in Gap's case:

◆ Productivity increased 21 percent.
◆ Quality increased 15 percent.
◆ Employee engagement increased 86 percent.
◆ Production turnover dropped by 50 percent.
◆ Work/life balance scores are at 82 percent.

An even more promising upside is to use the ROWE system to become the employer of choice. As Art Peck points out, "When we come out of this recession, we will be the only retailer in the Bay area that offers this competitive recruiting advantage. We're excited about that!"

Other companies are reaping the benefits of ROWE as well. For example, 40 percent of IBM's workforce has no official office. AT&T says one-third of all its managers are allowed to work from home, from their car, from the beach, or at Starbucks. Sun Microsystems will save $400 million in real estate costs (over six years) by allowing 50 percent of its employees to work from wherever they want.

Hire Back to the Future

Here is a contrarian idea that seems counterintuitive to those of us who are dedicated to future thinking. Hire old people. Seriously, did you know that by 2016 33 percent of the total U.S. workforce will be 50 years old or older? That's up from 28 percent in 2007. Smart organizations are attracting and retaining mature, experienced employees. This tactic is important for organizations that want to keep a competitive edge.

Since 2001, the AARP (American Association for Retired Persons) has published an annual list of the Best Employers for Workers Over 50. AARP wants to recognize "organizations that have implemented new and innovative policies and best practices to meet their talent management needs in the current economic environment."

Read those two paragraphs again and you'll weed out the phrases "retaining mature, experienced employees," and "organizations that want to keep a competitive edge" and "[hiring older workers meets a company's] talent management needs." How is that possible if most organizations must continue to innovate? Aren't older workers anxious to take early retirement "packages" so they can spend more time at the golf course or a day spa?

Brother, if that's what you think, then you don't know old people very well.

Thanks to medical science, men and women over 50 are feeling as physically and mentally effective as 30 year olds. The term "active senior" has wormed its way into our national lexicon to mean a person over 50 who still wants to be involved in sports and maintain a career. Thanks to the nosedive in the housing and stock markets, many seniors have to keep working.

And despite what you might think, older workers are more likely to innovate than their under-25 counterparts.

According to the Kauffman Foundation, the highest rate of entrepreneurship in America has shifted to the 55 to 64 age group, with people over 55 almost twice as likely to launch successful companies than those between 20 and 34. While this group may not invent the newest, sexiest iPad app, they bring years of experience and wisdom to their chosen start-ups. Take First Solar, for example. According to *Forbes* magazine's Fast Tech 500, First Solar was founded by a 68-year-old in 1984. The founders of Riverbed Technology, number two on the *Forbes* list, were 51 and 33 when they started their networking company. Even Zynga, the Internet company behind Farmville and other virally popular games, will likely zip past a billion dollars in revenue next year. The founder of Zynga is Mark Pincus. Is he your typical grad student genius? Hardly. Mark will have to face being 45 years old next year.

One of the most impressive (and innovative) examples of plucking brainpower from the retired talent pool happens at Northrop Grumman (NG), which is responsible for designing and building some of the most sophisticated combat aircraft in the world.

I spoke with John Gilpin, president of NG's Material Management group. Gilpin is in charge of many products in the fighter-plane group (B-2 bomber, F-5, T-38, Global Hawk). But his newest project is the F-35, which will replace the current state-of-the-art F-18. This next-generation fighter jet will have "Harrier" capabilities—meaning it can take off straight up—and will still be able to achieve supersonic airspeeds of more than 770 miles per hour.

To design a fighter plane this revolutionary, Gilpin had to band together the best minds in the business, and his considerable experience taught him where to find them. Gilpin told me, "I tracked down folks who worked at Northrop before, or worked on the B-2 program before, or worked on other programs but left our company and went to other companies or simply retired. I spread the word, 'Hey, do you know anybody who's got aircraft experience that we should draw on to beef up [the F-35 program]?' I want to get people who come highly recommended, who have the experience and the job knowledge, and who can pretty much just come on board and fit right in—get going right away. Many said, 'Oh, yeah. I'll come back [to Northrop].' These talented individuals wanted to come back because we are making exciting products here—history-making aircraft. And another thing: We make sure that employees are very happy with what we give them as far as benefits and wages. We are very proud of that."

And look at the financial advantages of rehiring this aging workforce. Their experience allows them to hit the ground running without a lot of "spooling up." They are willing (and excited) to work part time with flexible hours. They can often work from home so they don't take up office space and/or extra administrative costs. And if they don't work out, your downside risk is minimized.

Now, doesn't that kind of employment model match up with a progressive future thinking manager's talent management initiative? Yeah, that's what I thought, too.

Still not convinced something like ROWE might work for you? Still not sure hiring older people is wise? It's not my job to convince you. I'm just telling you what I see working for organizations that want to dominate during and after the recovery.

On the other hand, you can always let your competitors try it out and see what happens.

Homework

◆ Have you clearly defined the "best results" metric for each of your profit centers?
◆ Are you concerned your team would be less effective if they didn't work under your daily, visual supervision?
◆ Are your competitors adopting the ROWE method in any form?
◆ Is there a department or division in which you could safely test the ROWE method?

◆ Have you explored the cost/benefit comparisons of hiring older, experienced part-timers?

◆ Would you need to design a different metric to measure the performance of older workers; in order to minimize downside risk?

Last Words

I feel compelled to repeat the premise of this book: Your best shot at becoming one of the most successful organizations during the recovery phase of this current economy—and beyond—is to never forget that *the public* knows what they want. People know how they want it and when they want it. So listen carefully to them.

Don't ignore emerging trends (social and technological). Trends are the chatter talked about on TV, the web, and among friends. They are the big, burning, red flare the public sends up to tell you they are changing their habits and behavior.

If you ever find yourself at a crossroads of decision about your company, remember the immortal words of my father:

"It's always easier to ride the horse in the direction it's going."
—Chuck Shafer, 1927–2001

Backing Up These Outrageous Claims

CHAPTER 1

How McDonald's Took on Starbucks
www.reuters.com/article/2009/05/27/us-mcdonalds-idUSTRE54Q4L920090527

What Happened to Payless ShoeSource?
http://en.wikipedia.org/wiki/Payless_ShoeSource

Foot Locker Deleted 190 Locations
www.shoppingblog.com/blog/108109

Famous Footwear Gave Up Approximately 70 Stores
www.jsonline.com/blogs/business/84036882.html

Zappos Purchased by Amazon.com
http://techcrunch.com/2009/07/22/amazon-buys-zappos/

CHAPTER 2

NetFlix Didn't Sneak Up on Anybody
http://en.wikipedia.org/wiki/Netflix

Goodbye Hollywood Video
www.bizjournals.com/sacramento/stories/2007/10/15/daily23.html

http://latimesblogs.latimes.com/entertainmentnewsbuzz/2010/09/blockbuster-files-for-chapter-11-bankruptcy-sets-plan-to-reorganize.html

Napster's Rise and Fall
www.hometechanswers.com/mp3/history-of-napster.html

http://en.wikipedia.org/wiki/Napster

How Apple Won the Music War
http://lowendmac.com/orchard/05/origin-of-the-ipod
.html#1

Kodak Invented the Digital Camera—Then, Oops
www.msnbc.msn.com/id/9261340/ns/technology_
and_science-tech_and_gadgets/

The Digital Camera Players
www.dpreview.com/reviews/timeline.asp?start=1999

Kodak Tries to Play Catch-Up
www.dpreview.com/news/0401/04011301kodakfilm.asp

http://en.wikipedia.org/wiki/Eastman_Kodak

Remember Fotomat?
http://en.wikipedia.org/wiki/Fotomat

Kodak's Fall from Grace
www.numberof.net/number-of-kodak-employees/

SONY Still Doesn't Get the Book Content Right
www.fastcompany.com/1686283/sony-makes-e-readers-
touchy-takes-em-where-amazon-fears-to-tread

http://elab.eserver.org/hfl0014.html

Kindle Editions Outsell Print Books
www.webpronews.com/kindle-outsells-print-books-
says-amazon-2011-05

Borders Files for Bankruptcy
http://theweek.com/article/index/212130/borders-
goes-bankrupt-the-end-of-the-bookstore

CHAPTER 3

Customer Indifference Is a Terrible Strategy
http://ezinearticles.com/?How-Important-is-On-Demand-
Customer-Service-to-Your-Small-Business&id=1408562

Urgency versus Satisfaction
www.thinkcustomersatisfaction.com/2010/08/5-tips-to-maintain-urgency-and-improve.html

http://event.on24.com/eventRegistration/
EventLobbyServlet?target=lobby.jsp&playerwidth=950
&playerheight=680&totalwidt

http://blogs.forrester.com/jean_pierre_garbani

The Experience Economy
http://en.wikipedia.org/wiki/The_Experience_Economy

The Viral Fall of a Dictator
www.huffingtonpost.com/2011/02/11/egypt-facebook-revolution-wael-ghonim_n_822078.html

www.huffingtonpost.com/2011/02/11/mubarak-red-sea-egypt_n_821812.html

The Heavenly Bed Game Changer
www.conventionplanit.com/article.php?sid=3266

http://mybrc.myobnet.com/2011/02/15/heavenly-beds-at-the-westin-hotel/

CHAPTER 4

Christine Romans
www.usatoday.com/money/books/reviews/2010-10-25-smartrich25_ST_N.htm

Humble Leaders
www.i4cp.com/trendwatchers/2003/08/08/the-noble-humble-leader

Apple Pays App Builders $2 Billion
http://it-jobs.fins.com/Articles/SB129916354136891579/
The-Other-Apple-News-That-s-Great-for-Developers

Netflix Innovation Prize
http://en.wikipedia.org/wiki/Netflix_Prize

http://en.wikipedia.org/wiki/Netflix

Starbucks Splash Stick
www.usatoday.com/money/advertising/adtrack/2008-04-13-ad-track_N.htm?csp=N008

U-Test
www.utest.com/customers

GE's Ecomagination Contest
http://challenge.ecomagination.com/home

Boeing's 787 Dreamliner
http://answers.yahoo.com/question/index?
qid=20071113042059AAmA43N

www.bnet.com/article/for-boeing-it-takes-a-village-to-build-a-new-airplane/57965

Threadless T-Shirts
www.thecrowdsourcingblog.com/2010/09/success-stories-in-crowdsourcing-threadless-video/

http://en.wikipedia.org/wiki/Threadless

The Ultimate Customer Evaluation Question
www.theultimatequestion.com/theultimatequestion/home.asp

http://en.wikipedia.org/wiki/Net_Promoter

CHAPTER 5

Ramani Ayer at Hartford
http://en.wikipedia.org/wiki/Ramani_Ayer

Magnusson Klemencic Associates
www.mka.com/

Mortenson Construction

www.bizjournals.com/twincities/stories/2009/06/22/
focus1.html

www.mortenson.com/Profile_LeaderProfile_
TomGunkel.aspx

Daniel Pink

www.danpink.com/

Pete Winemiller

www.nba.com/thunder/news/gamenight_petewinemiller_
091211.html

CHAPTER 6

Groundlink Says *Yes*!

www.businessinsider.com/blackboard/revisions/
groundlink

http://boss.blogs.nytimes.com/2010/06/23/
how-i-saved-my-company-groundlink/

Recession Officially Starts

http://money.cnn.com/2008/12/01/news/economy/
recession/index.htm

PPG Automotive Paints

www.ppg.com/coatings/autooem/products/Pages/
default.aspx

PPG Innovates Waterborne Paint Finishes

www.ppg.com/coatings/autooem/about/Pages/default
.aspx

Ford Motor Company Makes a Comeback

www.businessweek.com/news/2010-01-29/ford-
forecasts-2010-profit-as-mulally-ends-three-annual-
losses.html

The Ritz-Carlton Catastrophe
www.reuters.com/article/2010/02/09/us-ritzcarlton-idUSTRE61850J20100209

AIG Effect and the Travel Industry
www.bnet.com/blog/travel/the-aig-effect-and-corporate-travel/742

www.walletpop.com/2009/03/09/the-aig-effect-luxury-travel-just-isnt-cool-anymore/

www.forbes.com/2010/02/16/aig-business-travel-leadership-meetings-10-corporate-conferences.html

www.nytimes.com/2009/02/01/opinion/01dowd.html

www.bloomberg.com/apps/news?pid=newsarchive&sid=a2FFCwEXuZhE&refer=news

www.nytimes.com/2009/03/18/opinion/l18aig.html

Hotel Demand Coming Back
www.procurement.travel/Smith-hotel-occupancy-revenue.2010081101

Neiman Marcus CEO Karen Katz Decides Who Will Be the Next Product Star
www.mccombs.utexas.edu/news/pressreleases/katz06.asp

Paris Hilton Eats While Soapy
www.youtube.com/watch?v=12t2z_G3Npg&feature=related

Padma Lakshmi Shouldn't Be Doing This with a Burger
www.youtube.com/watch?v=wNaB35-1x9M&feature=related

Kim Kardashian Doesn't Like to Get Messy
http://youtu.be/J11qUjHiGhs

The Charbroiled Turkey Burger Success
www.grubgrade.com/2011/03/24/fast-food-review-new-charbroiled-turkey-burger-from-carls-jr/

Miss Turkey Looks Good Poolside
http://youtu.be/vmTLAs6SyS4

Miss Turkey's Bikini
http://cgi.ebay.com/320696784064

The Cabot Hosiery Mills Sock Story
www.vermontguides.com/2006/11-nov/cobot_mills.html

www.lifeofall.com/31st-annual-cabot-hosiery-mills-sock-sale/

http://video.nytimes.com/video/2010/07/07/business/smallbusiness/1247468399140/darn-tough-vermont.html

Why Companies Take Risks during a Recession
http://economictimes.indiatimes.com/features/companies-willing-to-take-risks-in-a-recession/articleshow/4649683.cms

McGraw-Hill Advertising during a Recession
http://knowledge.wharton.upenn.edu/article.cfm?articleid=2101

http://thewomensjournal.com/20100405/advertising-and-promotion-during-a-recession-a-special-note-from-the-womens-journal/

Wells Fargo Gets Aggressive
http://dealbook.nytimes.com/2008/10/03/wells-fargo-to-merge-with-wachovia/

John Stumpf Rocks!
www.bizjournals.com/dayton/news/2011/03/21/wells-fargo-gives-19m-payday-ceo-stumpf.html

TD Bank Buys 1,000 Locations
www.mybanktracker.com/bank-news/2010/05/17/td-bank-acquires-the-south-financial-group-inc/

KB Toys Closes Up Shop
http://insidebutlercounty.com/index.php/local-sports/headlines/1733-kb-toys-to-shut-downlocal-store-affected

Toys "R" Us Rules the World
http://en.wikipedia.org/wiki/Toys_%22R%22_Us

www.bloomberg.com/apps/news?
pid=newsarchive&sid=aijAoDFBRLQE

http://en.wikipedia.org/wiki/Toy

Bold Move for ESPN
http://sports.espn.go.com/espn/wire?
section=soccer&id=5119202

www.espnmediazone3.com/us/2011/02/01/espn-
acquires-rights-to-2012-and-2016-uefa-european-
football-championship/

Valero the Visionary
www.nytimes.com/2009/03/19/business/energy-
environment/19ethanol.html

The EV1 Goes Away
http://en.wikipedia.org/wiki/General_Motors_EV1

http://news.yahoo.com/s/ap/20110308/ap_on_bi_ge/
as_japan_toyota_hybrid

CHAPTER 7

Diana Gray, Oracle Financial Strategies
http://blogs.oracle.com/mt/mtsearch.cgi?
blog_id=47&tag=Oracle&limit=20

ROWE in Action
http://gorowe.com/

www.danpink.com/archives/2008/08/rowe

www.businessweek.com/magazine/content/06_50/
b4013001.htm

www.businessweek.com/careers/managementiq/
archives/2009/09/gap_to_employee.html

www.hrmreport.com/article/Getting-the-Right-Results/

www.govloop.com/profiles/blogs/how-ibm-does-the-results

http://blog.seattlepi.com/workplacewrangler/2010/03/27/is-rowe-the-best-form-of-employee-engagement/

Employers Bringing Back Boomers
http://money.usnews.com/money/careers/articles/2009/10/05/the-best-employers-for-older-workers?PageNr=2

AARP Best Employers for People Over 50
www.newsweek.com/2010/08/20/innovation-grows-among-older-workers.html

www.aarp.org/work/employee-benefits/best_employers/

Older Workers Innovate
www.newsweek.com/2010/08/20/innovation-grows-among-older-workers.html

About the Author

Ross Shafer is in high demand as a keynote speaker on the subjects of innovation, market share growth, customer urgency, and fresh leadership practices. Ross has written and produced 14 human resources training films and also founded the Customer Empathy Institute in conjunction with California State University at Monterey Bay. He is the author of the books *Nobody Moved Your Cheese,*
The Customer Shouts Back, Customer Empathy, Are You Relevant?, and oddly enough, *Cook-Like-A-Stud: 38 Lip-Smackin' Meals Men Can Cook in the Garage . . . Using Their Own Tools!*

Before he started writing and speaking about shifting buying habits and contrarian leadership principles, Ross was an Emmy Award–winning network television host and comedian. He hosted *The Late Show* on Fox, *Days End* on ABC, *Almost Live* on NBC, *Love Me Love Me Not* on USA, and *The Match Game* for ABC. So when Ross gives a speech it is always hilarious, energizing, and enlightening.

To contact Ross directly, go to www.RossShafer.com.